Get Going on the Internet

PRENTICE HALL EUROPE

London New York Toronto Sydney Tokyo Singapore
Madrid Mexico Munich Paris

First published 1998 by
Prentice Hall Europe
Campus 400, Maylands Avenue
Hemel Hempstead
Hertfordshire, HP2 7EZ
A division of
Simon & Schuster International Group

© Prentice Hall 1998

All rights reserved. No part of this publication may be reproduced, stored in a retrieval system, or transmitted, in any form, or by any means, electronic, mechanical, photocopying, recording or otherwise, without prior permission, in writing, from the publisher.

Typeset in 9.5/12 Bookman Light
by PPS, London Road, Amesbury, Wilts.

Printed and bound in Great Britain by
T.J. International Ltd, Padstow, Cornwall

Library of Congress Cataloging-in-Publication Data

Get Going on the Internet.
    p. cm.
   Includes index.
   ISBN 0-13-737891-2
    1. Internet (Computer network)
TK5105.875.I57B764 1996   96-48477
004.67′8—dc21   CIP

British Library Cataloguing in Publication Data

A catalogue record for this book is available from
the British Library

ISBN 0-13-737891-2

1 2 3 4 5   02 01 00 99 98

Contents

Chapter 1 Is the Internet for you?   1
What is the Internet?   1
Why People Use the Net – what's in it for you?   4
History of the Net   6

Chapter 2 The parts that make up the Internet   8
Definition of the Bits   8
The World Wide Web   9
Newsgroups and Usenet   11
E-mail   13
Online Services   15
Gaming and IRC   17

Chapter 3 What you need to start   19
Modems   20
ISDN   21
Leased Lines   22
Internet Cafés   22
Tech Box: Modems   23

Tech Box: ISDN and Leased Lines 25
Connecting the Modem to your PC 26
Tech Box: Watch Out for Older PCs (and their UARTs) 27
The UART (Universal Asynchronous Receiver Transmitter) Chip 28
Internet Browsers 28

Chapter 4 Your computer hardware – what you need 31
The Global View 32
The Processor 33
Processor Upgrade 35
Memory 36
Hard Disk 36
Video 37
MPEG Video 39
Monitor 40
Audio 41
Still Worried? 42

Chapter 5 How does the software work? 43
Anatomy of a Browser 43
Anatomy of a News Reader 45
Anatomy of a an E-mail Reader 46

Chapter 6 It's in the post 48
How Do I Send Mail? 49
What Does an E-mail Address Mean? 50
Where Do I find Someone's E-mail Address? 51
   Bigfoot 51
   Deja News 52
   LookUp 52
   Four11 52
   E-mail Someone you Don't Know 52

Chapter 7 Usenet – the Internet speakeasy 54
Newsgroups 54
Usenet Discussion 55
How Does Usenet Work? 56

Posting a Message   56
Responding to Other Messages   58
Exploring Usenet   59
It's Not for the Nervous   60
Some Newsgroups to get you Started   61
  Computing   61
  Hobbies   61
  Sport   62
  UK-Specific   62
  Trivial but Amusing   62
  Business   63
  Jokes, Japes, Funny Business   63
  Images   64

Chapter 8 Getting caught in the Web   65
We're Off   66
How Do I Browse?   68

Chapter 9 Search engines – searching for places to go   71
  Yahoo! UK & Ireland   74
  AltaVista   74
  Electric Library   74
  Lycos   75
  Magellan   75
  A2Z   75
The Best of the Rest   76
  Amazing Environmental Organization Webdirectory   76
  Argus/University of Michigan Clearinghouse   76
  Shareware.com   76
  Deja News   76
  Excite   77
  Gamelan   77
  GNN Select   77
  G.O.D.   77
  Hotbot   78
  IBM Infomarket   78
  Infoseek Guide   78
  Nerdworld Media Internet Subject Index   78
  100 Hot Websites   78

Open Text Index   79
Point   79
Starting Point   79
Webcrawler   79
W3 Servers   79
What's New   79
Whowhere?   79

Chapter 10 Suggested Web sites   80
Books   91
   Internet Bookshop   91
   Internet Public Library   91
   Books On-Line   91
   HarperCollins Interactive   92
   Internet Talking Bookshop   92
   Prentice Hall   92
   Amazon.com   92
   Spawn   92
   Travel Books   93
   Philip K. Dick   93
   Pulp Faction   93
Business and money   93
   Loot   93
   Shoppers Universe   93
   Investor's Edge   93
   Reuter's Business Headlines   94
   FT.com   94
   Wall Street Journal   94
   UK Business Index   94
   People Bank   94
   Résumé writing   95
   MoneyWorld UK   95
Comedy   95
   Joke of the day   95
   ComedyWeb   95
   Pythonline   95
   Wall-o-shame   96
   Migraine Boy   96
   Carry On   96
   Light Bulb Jokes   96

Contents

   The Secret Diary of Bill Gates 96
   Ask Mr Angst 96
   Dear Xavier Landers 96
Computing 97
   UK Internet Directory 97
   Shareware.com 97
   ZDNet 97
   Versions 97
   Microsoft 98
Culture 98
   National Museum of Film, Photography and
      Television 98
   Smithsonian Institution 98
   The Louvre 99
   Literary Calendar 99
Shakespeare and the Globe 99
   UK Club Map 99
Education 99
   New Scientist 99
   Discovery Channel Online 100
   Internet for Learning 100
   Educate Online 100
   Interactive Frog Dissection 100
   NUS Online 100
   Arachnomania 100
Employment 101
   Online Career Centre 101
   CareerWeb 101
   CareerNet UK 101
   Gradunet 101
   Jobs in the UK 101
Games 102
   The Games Domain 102
   Entertainment Online 102
   Id Software 102
   Riddler 102
   Gamespot 102
Government 103
   The Labour Party 103
   The Conservative Party 103

Contents

  The Liberal Democratic Party   103
  CCTA Government Information   103
  The White House   103
  No. 10 Downing Street   103
Music   104
  NME.com   104
  MTV Online   104
  Atlantic Records   104
  Pathfinder   104
  Classic CD   104
  Pastel Blue   105
  CD World   105
  Spin Magazine   105
  Virgin Radio   105
  Internet Beatles album and Beatles info   105
Newspapers   105
  MSNBC   105
  Electronic Telegraph   106
  PA News   106
  CNN Interactive   106
  The Times   106
  Electronic Newstand   106
  Guardian OnLine   106
Personals   107
  Dateline UK   107
  Cupid's Network   107
  Match.com   107
Radio, Film and TV   107
  Cyberville Radio   107
  Interactive TV Guide   107
  Paramount Pictures   108
  Star Trek   108
  Internet Movie database   108
  Mr Showbiz   108
  Channel 4   109
  Cinemania OnLine   109
Religion   109
  A Christian Introduction to the Web   109
  WWW Bible Gateway   109
  Man is Man Made   109

Contents

   Comparative Religion   109
   Vatican Radio   110
   Spirit-WWW   110
Sport   110
   World Sports Report   110
   FIFA Online   110
   ESPN SportZone   110
   Soccernet   111
   Sydney 2000   111
   Sports Chat!   111

Chapter 11 You want software? We got software – downloading   112
Some history: Why you Can Get Software for Free   113
Let's Go and Find Some Software Then   114
   The Easy Way   114
   The Hard(er) Way   115
Where's the Catch?   116
   Dr Solomon's   117
   McAfee VirusScan   118
   Norton AntiVirus   118
Some FTP Sites to Get You Started   118
   CU-SeeMe   118
   F-Prot   118
   HotDog   118
   VMPeg   118

Chapter 12 You can broadcast too   119
Email   120
Mailing lists   122
   Joining a Mailing List   123
Newsgroups   124
IRC   125
Internet Telephony and Videoconferencing   128

Chapter 13 Making your own page   130
What Do I Do?   130
What Do I Put on My Pages?   131
How Do Web Pages Work?   132

Introducing HTML   133
Getting Started with HTML   134
Add A Title and Text   135
Be Bold (Or Be Italic . . .)   138
Insert Links To Other Sites   138
   Links To Pages On Your Own Site   140
Let's Get Colourful!   141
A Few HTML Tips   143
Short cuts   144
Five Don'ts and Five Do's for Web Pages   144

Chapter 14 Netiquette for beginners   146
Basic Netiquette   147
   Newsgroups   147
   E-mail Netiquette   149
   A word about spam   149
Smileys, Abbreviations and the World of Emoticons   150
Smileys   151
A Small Dictionary of Smileys   152

Chapter 15 Net myths and reality   153
Are There Really No Laws on the Internet?   153
Is the Net Full of Pornography?   154
Content Filters   155
Can a Hacker Get Access to My Computer?   158
I'm a Woman – Will I be Sexually Harassed if I Go
   Online?   159
I Can Buy Anything I Want on the Web   159
Will I get Addicted to the Net and Run Up a Huge
   Phone Bill?   160
Offline Browsing for Beginners   161
   NearSite   162
   Browser Buddy   162
   Secret Agent   162
Isn't There Going to be a Special £500 Computer for
   Net Access?   162

Glossary   163

Index   173

CHAPTER 1

Is the Internet for you?

You've heard about it, you've seen adverts for it – but what is it?

The following sections will try and answer that for you and give you an idea as to whether the Internet is for you. First, 'What is the Internet?' gives a simple explanation of what you are looking at, then we take a look at 'Why People Use the Net: What's in it for you?' Some of the things you are likely to find and some ideas what you can do with the Internet. The chapter is rounded off with a 'History of the Net'.

What is the Internet?

This is a question a lot of people don't like to ask because they are afraid the answer is going to be far too difficult to understand: and when you look at some of the explanations

CHAPTER 1 ▽ Is the Internet for you?

that are being given it would seem a reasonable fear. This is a great shame, because while there *are* some appallingly complicated processes taking place when you connect to it, the Internet itself isn't a difficult thing to understand. For the time being, however, just to get you ready to understand what the Internet is, you might start to limber up your imagination by thinking of libraries and motorways.

The problem of describing the Internet is compounded because the Internet doesn't exist in a physical way. It doesn't, for example, live in a big darkened room with 'Internet' written on the door, and this means that there are no easy-to-understand photographs or drawings to use when describing it. Instead we rely on metaphors.

And in this case, as you may have guessed, it is a metaphor involving roads and libraries. When you see what the Internet really is you are likely to be surprised how simple it is, so you may want to sit down at this point. Are you sitting comfortably? Right, imagine a road map. It covers the country (or the world if you like) and it has motorways and A roads and B roads and anything else that'll take a car. Anywhere you want to go you can get to by road. If you have a place on the map that doesn't have a road going to it, you make a road: it can be a motorway or a dirt track, it doesn't matter; what you are doing is connecting that place up to the road network so that you and others can visit it.

That is the physical side of the Internet, it is that simple: anywhere on the map is available to you. The roads are the equivalent of the links between the computers on the net (and don't forget computers store information – keep thinking of libraries). In reality these roads are the world's telephone systems: that is why it is so easy to 'build' a link; it is simply connecting up to a telephone line.

And just like the road network, if a road is closed you can usually get where you want to go by taking a diversion. If the M1 is shut there are lots of other roads you can travel on, it gets a bit congested, but you *do* get there. This is exactly like the Internet, if a link breaks between one computer and another there is usually another route you can take to the same place.

Now we get onto the libraries. As you look at a map of roads you see that at each intersection where the roads connect there is a little blob. Imagine this blob as a little library. On the Internet this blob is a computer, and the computer contains the information that is being shared across the net – there are millions of computers on the Internet all around the world, each one supplying another bit of information. Each is connected to the phone and can be accessed by anyone and everyone on the Net.

So you have these links to these little libraries making up a giant library that reaches across the world. It doesn't matter that it really consists of computers and telephones, what matters is the information in these little libraries. Anyone (including you) can put information onto the Internet, and you are perfectly at liberty to enhance the library with whatever information you like.

On these computers is the information that the other people on the Internet want to share with you and the rest of the world. This information can be anything from photographs of their dog, to synopses of *NYPD Blue*, right over to discussions on your favourite author and an explanation as to how to play Led Zeppelin's 'The Rain Song' on guitar (including the correct tuning).

And, of course, this is a haven for anyone interested in *Star Trek* (although don't worry if you aren't interested in *Star Trek*, the place is big enough to wander around without ever seeing so much as a whisper of it). Perhaps it is going a bit far to say 'all human knowledge' is there, but certainly most of the chapter headings are covered, and as new people join they add their own experiences and the whole thing grows and grows.

CHAPTER 1 ▽ Is the Internet for you?

In the early 1990s the US Vice President Al Gore coined the phrase 'The Information Superhighway'. As a phrase it doesn't mean much and in lots of ways has done much to confuse the issue as to what the Internet and, indeed, The Information Superhighway, is. But it carries the one word that helps define the Internet: Information. It is information that makes the Internet so special.

And this is why it is so popular. Currently figures suggest there are around 50 million people on the Internet world wide, and that figure is growing every day. If you decide to join you will be joining a group of people that are developing the communications of the future. This is where the future is happening.

Why People Use the Net: What's in it for you?

Too often people ignore what the Net can do for them before they jump on board – it doesn't take too long for most of them to find out, but there are some that miss the good stuff and leave disappointed. This is a bad thing because the Internet may be many things – some not all good – but disappointing it should never be.

Fundamentally the Internet is an enormous interactive library. Imagine a single library that is kept up to date by over 40 million people spread across the world. You can ask a question and get an answer from an expert (and then you can get another expert to explain the answer to you). You can even help other people by answering their questions.

You can go to different sites on the Web and find out about things you didn't know existed. You can meet people from all over the world – make new friends and catch up with old ones. You can hear music and watch TV, all via the Internet.

▽ Why People Use the Net   5

Of course you can also tell the world all about yourself. If you want to publish that book that has been sitting in the attic (or, indeed, in the back of your mind) for years, you can publish it on the Internet. Perhaps, if you can't think of an ending, you can ask others to suggest one – or maybe even write it for you. Currently Net users are discovering new ways to use their new toy – anything from starting a club that anyone can join to opening art galleries to show off their photographs.

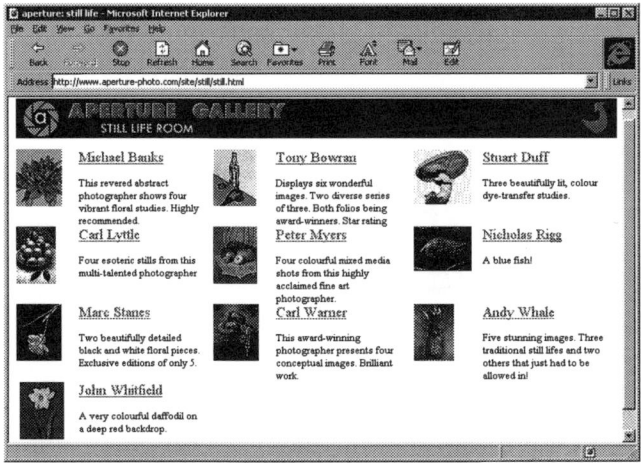

**One of those many photographic galleries, at
http://www.aperture-photo.com**

You can run your business over the Net; you can even use the Net as the foundation of your business. More and more companies have web pages that either show off their wares or allow you to buy goods there and then. Magazines have discovered the Net too, and are publishing special issues specifically for the Internet – some are even publishing Internet-specific magazines: a magazine you *can't* buy at the newsagents.

Its a bit like the old Wild West. The Internet is there to be tamed and turned into what you want. Whether it is just watching other people do their thing or making people watch while you do yours, the Internet is the perfect platform.

History of the Net

Like so many of the things we use, the Internet came about as a result of work for the defence industry. Back in July 1968 a part of the US Department of Defense, the Advanced Research Projects Agency (ARPA), asked for suggestions on how to connect four computer sites so that it could test the theory that a link could be sustained to the others if one was blown up during a war.

At the time people were already experimenting with linking computers over the telephone system and ARPA wanted to see if computers in different locations could be linked using a new technology known as packet switching. This is where data, before it is sent to another computer, is broken up into pieces – called a packet – then given an identifier and forwarding address and sent on its way. When it arrives it is a simple job to reassemble the data: hey presto, a data transfer mechanism. Ironically ARPA's goal was not the creation of today's Internet, but merely a data network that could survive a nuclear attack.

The system allowed computers to share data and, most importantly, allowed the researchers working on the project to exchange electronic mail, or e-mail. E-mail was a revolution, it offered the ability to send detailed letters at the speed of a phone call and is probably the single most important thing to come from the research simply because it provided the interest in the project and the subsequent research to bring the Internet into the public domain. The term Internet (from 'internetworking') can be traced back to a 1974 planning document and by the 1980s it had stuck.

Thirty years after the first experiment it is possibly one of the single biggest technologies to come to the human race and it

History of the Net

is still growing. Everybody seems to be getting in on the act. It is interesting to note that during the Gulf War Iraq kept its lines of communication open – despite the allies' best efforts – by using the Internet. Of course the people at ARPA are bound to be very proud.

Currently the Internet has 50 million users and is growing: that's enough for a small country – only this is a 'country' that spans the world.

CHAPTER 2
The parts that make up the Internet

Definition of the Bits

Having given a rough picture of what the Internet is, we're now going to tell you what you get for your money. We'll be looking at

- The World Wide Web
- Newsgroups and Usenet
- E-mail
- Online services
- Gaming and IRC

All these subjects will be more closely looked at later on in the book; this is just a taster to put you in the picture and get you started.

The World Wide Web

The 'World Wide Web' or 'W3' or 'The Web' is the colourful bit of the Internet. A couple of years ago it hardly existed, but now it is what a lot of newcomers believe the Internet to be, although while it is certainly the biggest growing sector it certainly isn't the only part.

The Web is graphical (that is, it has pictures) and was originally meant for simply looking at, although that has grown much more into 'interacting with' these days. Nowadays the Web has sound pictures and animation – and is often described by the M word: Multimedia (which really means 'comes with added sound and pictures' – the Internet doesn't have smell yet).

So, the Web is like a picture book – a single picture on the Web is called a page – and this really is the best way to think of it. As likely as not it will have a title, text and some sort of picture. Most people who have a presence on the Web can create their own Web pages and, of course, they can be about anything you want.

Anything. For example, if you were a fan of *Starsky and Hutch* (which, for our younger readers, is a 1970s US TV cop show) you might want to put a page on the Web for other fans – but take note, it has already been done. Or you might want to create a page for caving enthusiasts (again, it has been done). In other words your pages are only limited by your imagination, while it is almost as fascinating a journey simply discovering other people's imagination.

CHAPTER 2 ▽ The parts that make up the Internet

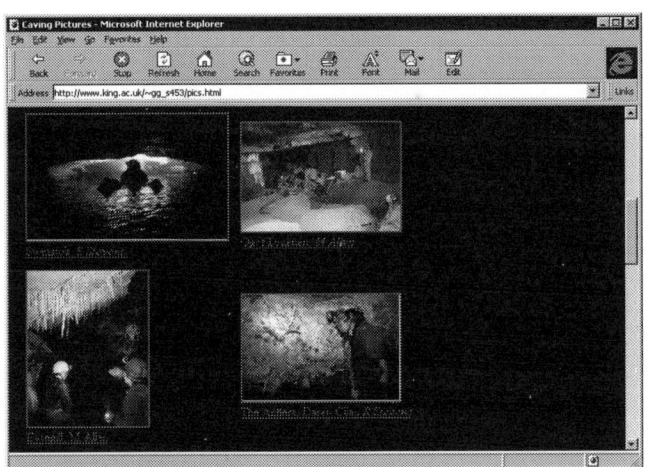

The Kingston University Caving Club at http://www.king.ac.uk/~gg_s463/

Getting around the Web is very much like going visiting friends. You have an address (called by the 'techies' a URL, or Uniform Resource Locator) of a site that has some interesting 'stuff' on it, which might be, say, the Murray Walker quotes page. You type its address into your special Internet visiting software (called a browser) and off you go. The address of the Murray Walker page is `http://www.users.zenet.co.uk/petef/racing/walkerisms.html`. Your computer connects to the other computer at that address and looks for the data that is available, then it displays what it finds on the screen.

Voilà, you are surfing the net. On the page you will find buttons known as hot links, and they will either move you on to another page on the site you are visiting or move you miles away to another site. Usually the other sites that are linked to the one you are visiting are deemed by the author of the page to be interesting; thus your journey continues.

If you want you can search for what you are looking for (or, just idly search on the first thing you think of). We shall be looking at search engines later, but to give an example of what you might find, if you typed 'gere' you would discover that there is a site that is dedicated to Richard Gere:

▽ **Newsgroups and Usenet**

Click on the picture to learn more about Richard Gere's films

http://www.pair.com/marilynn/gere.htm. As a research resource there isn't much, if anything, that can beat it.

Some of these sites have sound clips or animated pictures on them and you will be able to put sound and animation on your page. There are no rules as to what you should do (which is both good and bad of course), but it is always different. We shall be talking further about the Web later in the book.

Newsgroups and Usenet

If the Web is the colourful bit of the Internet, then newsgroups are the monochrome part. Newsgroups were the first part of the Net to develop and, as such, are almost as old as the Net itself. To understand a newsgroup, first think of a notice board on a village green.

Standing there by the duck pond at the centre of the village everyone can see it. One morning someone puts a post-it note on the board which says 'Did you see TV last night?'.

CHAPTER 2 ▽ The parts that make up the Internet

Curious, a passer-by puts a post-it note underneath the first saying 'Did I see what on TV last night?'. A bit later on the first poster puts another message under the second one saying 'the big film'. Now, a third person comes along, notices the conversation going on and chips in, 'Yeah, I saw it. Great wasn't it?'

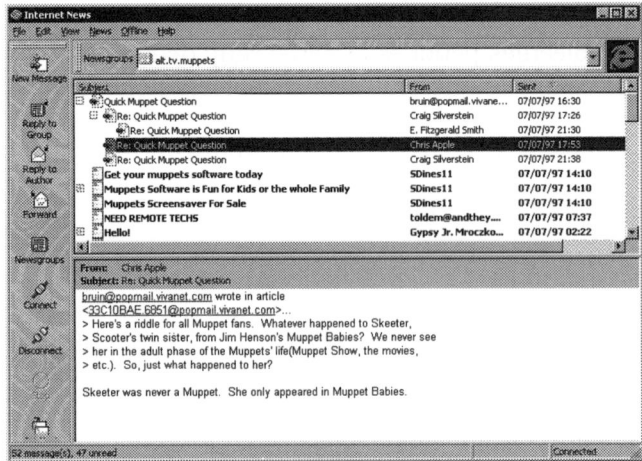

The place to hold those vital Muppet conversations!

This is effectively what happens in newsgroups, hundreds of people all looking at the same notice board and reading the various messages posted on it. If the message is interesting or asks for information that the reader has, he or she posts a reply and a conversation starts. Anyone else can join, and just like the notice board on the village green it can be ignored when it is boring and joined when it is interesting.

But it isn't just one notice board.

More than 25 000 of these conversation points exist – generating over 50 000 postings every day. That's a lot of information. Each newsgroup has a specific topic to cover, so anything from scuba diving to guitar music and people post messages one after the other – just like the village notice board – every day. The newsgroups can be news oriented or hobby oriented, some of the content can be a bit saucy – some downright rude – and a lot of it is just people talking about subjects that matter to them.

The names sound a bit strange but there is logic behind them: alt.music.led-zeppelin is an appreciation of the rock group Led Zeppelin, while, if that is a bit extreme for your tastes bionet.molecules.peptides (a newsgroup dedicated to examining the chemical and biological aspects of peptides) might be the one, or misc.writing.screenplays (all aspects of writing and selling screenplays) might be what you want.

Whatever the case, there is one there for your tastes.

You may have heard the term bulletin board system or BBS: this is same thing on a global scale. These are the places where you can contact experts in different fields – anything from problems with your car to medical advice. Experienced Internet users will find the place where some specialists hang out and then ask their questions. More often than not they will get more than one reply.

This system of newsgroups is called Usenet and has been going for over 15 years now – hence its size. The thing to remember about newsgroups is that you can't read them all. It is very important to be very precise about the groups you join or you will spend 95 per cent of your time wading through messages that have no relevance to you, and you will quickly get bored. Don't forget we shall be talking more about newsgroups later in the book.

E-mail

First things first: no, your postman doesn't deliver your e-mail. E-mail is electronic mail, and is perhaps the most

CHAPTER 2 ▽ The parts that make up the Internet

powerful tool of the Internet. It enables you to send a letter that can arrive almost instantaneously and receive a reply straight away – but, better still, it enables you to send a letter that will be picked up when the person it is addressed to is ready.

If you were sending a letter to the United States, you would expect it to take anything up to a week – sometimes longer. A phone call has to take in the time differences, so you are working out what is five hours behind our time for the East Coast and minus seven hours for the West Coast – so you call anyway and the person you want is either asleep or out.

The beauty of e-mail is when the person logs on to the Internet your mail is waiting for them, and their reply to you is waiting for you when you next look. Not quite instantaneous, but certainly efficient.

E-mail has grown immensely over the past couple of years and now offers many more features. Simply, electronic mail is a letter that you write on your computer and send via the Internet. It doesn't have a stamp or an envelope and it probably isn't quite as reliable as a letter we would post but it *is* convenient.

These days, in line with other developments on the Internet, you can send sounds and pictures with your e-mail, so the world is your oyster – or post box. So, if someone else is on the Internet then you can e-mail them. E-mail is also useful for putting out (and receiving) information. If there is a document you need to send to a handful of people you can send it to all of them at the same time. You just put their addresses at the front of the message and hit the send button.

It is also nice to know that you can often send e-mail to people who *aren't* on the Internet. This is because a lot of companies' computer networks are 'sort of' connected to the Internet, which means its users can send and receive e-mail sent via the Internet but can't actually surf it.

▽ **Online Services**

You will see e-mail addresses all around; they are the ones that have the '@' sign in the middle of what looks like gobbledegook. Thus chris@somewhere.co.uk could be an e-mail address: the bit at the front is the identity of the person who is sending it, and the bit after the @ is the system (or Internet Provider) it is coming from. More on e-mail later.

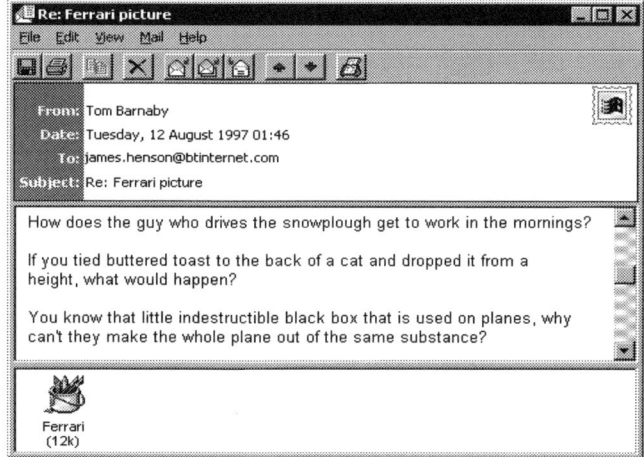

An e-mail message, with the recipient's address in the **To:** field

Online Services

When is the Internet not the Internet? When it is an online service. If you imagine the Internet as a computer jungle with connections everywhere, no rules and no one in charge, then online services are well-regulated clearings with fences up to stop the Internet getting in.

US Companies like CompuServe (CSi), America OnLine (AOL), Microsoft Network (MSN) and British companies like

CHAPTER 2 ▽ The parts that make up the Internet

Compulink Information Exchange (CIX) all provide Newsgroups like services that are regulated or, in the parlance, Moderated. This means if someone is being anti-social or rude a moderator will come along and sort it out.

CompuServe's all-in-one software makes its service simple to navigate

Each has its own 'feel' and has a different piece of software to access it. They all provide e-mail access so you can e-mail to and from them across the Internet.

Obviously you pay more for this service. While there is more organization in the forums and conferences (the equivalent titles for newsgroups) there aren't quite the broad number of subjects covered in them. Interestingly, people like Microsoft used to run a 'help' forum on CompuServe where its technical support staff would answer users' questions about its products; now they are moving that to the Internet so that more users can have access.

Most of these services provide access to the Internet, usually reached by just clicking on a button in your software, but despite the moderated conferences these systems are an

▽ **Gaming and IRC** 17

expensive way to get on the Internet and are best for people who want a more controlled environment.

Gaming and IRC

Do you want to meet people, make friends, have a laugh, get angry and do it all now? Then you must check out IRC or Internet Relay Chat. IRC is just like CB radio: you talk to a number of people but in 'Real Time' (which is a computer term for 'happening right now – in front of you'). You type in a comment, it appears on other people's machine as you type and someone else types in a response (don't worry if your typing is slow, everyone is slow to start with – and we all get faster).

There are different 'channels' that you can get on to and each will have a different discussion, and, of course, just like CB, it isn't regulated, so it is only as much fun as the people on it. This also means the conversation can be far ranging and erudite or very very local and simple; you simply choose what conversation you want to be part of.

Microsoft's Comic Chat lets you adopt different characters and emotions as you chat

CHAPTER 2 ▽ The parts that make up the Internet

It's worth mentioning that, because IRC is in 'Real Time', you are on the phone for as long as you are chatting – so it can get rather expensive.

For those of you who like to play games there are many places to go. For example, there are word puzzle sites, or online soap operas that allow you to tell the characters what to do. But probably the most organized games are the MUDs. This isn't the mud you might find in a field, but a Multi-User Dungeon, which is an online version of the old Dungeons and Dragons game.

The object in these games is to gain experience points so you can advance through the different levels. There is even a MUD game based on the *Star Trek* universe and MUDs for children.

CHAPTER 3

What you need to start

Ok, you have decided that you *are* going to make a go of the Internet; what now?

In this chapter we shall tell you about the hardware and software you will need to get on line. That means sections on ways of getting connected, where we talk about 'Modems', 'ISDN', 'Leased Lines' and 'Internet Cafés'. We then introduce our '*Tech Box*': this is a technical explanation of modems, ISDN and leased lines. If you have no interest in the technical aspect ignore this section (although you may well find it comes in useful later).

After that there is 'Connecting the Modem to Your PC', which is a brief description of where the bits plug in. There will also be a Tech Box for those of you interested in the innards of the PC (namely the UART chip). Then there is 'Internet Browsers' – the software that you use to look at the Internet.

CHAPTER 3 ▽ What you need to start

Modems

The word modem is made up from two words: MOdulator DEModulator, which, if you have a degree in double Dutch, tells you exactly what a modem does, but if you are like the rest of us it tells you absolutely nothing. It helps to understand what a modem has to do when describing it; simply it has to convert the language that the computer speaks into sounds that can be transmitted across telephone lines. And *then* it converts the stuff that is transmitted across telephone lines back into the language the computer speaks.

The point of modems is that they talk to other modems via telephone lines, and while they talk they are exchanging data. And if you have ever dialled a fax machine and heard it squeal at you then you have heard the sort of noise that a modem makes. Thus, modulator (converting from computer speak to telephone noise) demodulator (converting back from telephone noise to computer speak).

As the modem sits between your computer and the telephone line you'll be pleased to know that attaching it to your telephone system is simplicity itself. All you need is a spare phone socket – or if you don't have a spare, one of those 'two into one' phone sockets, available from most electrical shops, will do perfectly – and it will do all the talking to the outside world for you.

At the other end it is a little more complicated. If you wish you can have your modem inside your PC, and while this is easily the neatest approach to the subject it does require you to take the lid off and fiddle with your computer's innards – not something that a lot of newcomers relish doing.

For those that are a touch squeamish about playing with the insides of computers you can buy an external modem that connects to your computer's serial port (more on those a little later). This is very useful for non-technical types, but it is worth noting that an external device costs a little more – but, what price peace of mind?

▽ **ISDN**

There are lots of different types of modem you can buy, but it is a general rule of thumb that you should buy the fastest you can afford. By 'speed' we mean the *amount* of data transferred in a given time.

For example, in the old days (which for personal computers is less than 15 years ago) it was common to have a modem that ran at 300 Baud. This was more or less 300 bps, or bits per second. (There is a lot of discussion over the term Baud vs bits per second, but for the purpose of this book we can consider them the same.)

Speed is an issue because it is one of the factors that defines how quickly the Net appears on your computer. The faster you can download the data from the other end of the line the quicker it appears on your screen. And given the massive amount of data on the Net, the faster is always better (although it is worth noting that if you go online in the morning you miss the slight – but noticeable – slowing of the Internet caused by the whole of America all going online at once in the afternoon – their morning).

Nowadays you shouldn't consider buying a modem any slower than 28 800 bps. Although you can find very cheap 14 400 bps modems, they are a false economy unless you intend only to use e-mail. Recent increases in speed have given us the 33 600 (which costs much the same as the 28 800) and the ultra-fast 56 600 bps.

ISDN

ISDN stands for Integrated Services Digital Network, and is a sort of Big Boys computing technology. Essentially it is an industrial strength link to the Internet that is much faster than using a simple modem. The connection is installed just like a standard phone line, and you plug your equipment in much as you would as if it were an ordinary connection.

CHAPTER 3 ▽ What you need to start

The big advantage of ISDN is that it is already digital, so your computer doesn't need to convert its digital signals into an audio signal and pump it down the line, it just talks normally (more or less). This means you don't need a modem; the device that sits on the PC is called a terminal adaptor, and just like the modem you can have this external or internal.

The line being digital means you can get data coming down the line at a reasonably staggering 64 000 bps. But it is important to point out that unless you have some *very* specific needs you aren't going to need this much data this quickly (one of the other uses for ISDN is video conferencing).

ISDN may come to the home at some time in the future but at the moment it is really only businesses that can use it. It should only be considered if you intend to do some serious Web browsing, and if you consider this route, BT will be happy to talk to you about it.

Leased Lines

A leased line is literally a special telephone line that you rent from your telephone provider that is permanently connected to another telephone (or in this case an Internet Service Provider). You can get very high speeds through a leased line – and there is little chance of it ever being engaged.

Like ISDN a leased line is really a business solution and costs thousands and thousands of pounds a year, so there is very little a normal home user could do to justify the need for one.

Internet Cafés

The Internet Café is a relatively new invention and really quite useful if you really aren't sure if you want to get on line – only go to an Internet Café if you are prepared to be bewitched by the Net.

Tech Box: Modems

Cyberia, a popular chain of Internet cafés, has a home on the Web at http://www.cyberiacafe.net/

Find your nearest Internet Café and go along. They, in return for a couple of pounds, will either give you coffee or let you use one of their PCs that are connected to the Internet (or both). You can surf the Net and get a 'feel' for it – some of them even offer training.

These are great places to look before you buy, but tend to work out rather expensive if used *instead* of your own Internet account at home.

Tech Box: Modems

The modem's job is to get data from one part of the Internet to the other; it is as simple as that. That means looking at what makes up the data: data bits.

Without getting too technical it is worth pointing out that the smallest data character in the computer is a byte which is 8 bits wide. In this sense 'data character' can refer to any bit of computer information: a computer instruction or data (data is a computer term for information). To put it into perspective, this means that at 300 bits per second the maximum number of characters (each character being made up of 8 bit bytes)

CHAPTER 3 ▽ What you need to start

you can transfer in a second would be 37.5. And don't forget, if the data you were transmitting was a page of text you would have to include spaces, commas and full stops. In other words, less than a quarter the length of this paragraph in one second.

When you buy a modem you will be confronted by a myriad numbers starting with 'V'. They aren't a foreign language but are the standards that define the performance of the modem. The fastest speed isn't the only speed it runs at, a modem link is only as fast as the slowest modem on the link. If there is a modem at one end that only runs at 14 400 bps and the other one does 28 800 bps, then the link will be made at 14 400 and the faster modem will have to run more slowly; this slower speed is called a fallback speed.

At the moment you should be looking to buy a V.34 modem, which is a 28 800 bps modem (you may also see this written as V.fc, which is a similar standard offering more fallback speeds) or you may get a good deal on a V.34bis modem which runs at 33 600 bps.

The other side of the 'getting more data down the line' equation is compression. This is squeezing the data so there is less of it to go down the line, and enables the modem to shovel more information to the receiving end. V.42bis is a common compression standard that gives up to 4 : 1 compression.

Alas, as you try to get more data along the phone system, things like crackly lines and other noises cause problems and the data you are transferring gets corrupted. To solve this, a lot of modems have error-correcting circuitry built into them, where they monitor the data being sent and if there is a problem at the other end a signal is sent back requesting the information again.

The V.42bis compression standard also includes the V.42 error correction standard which is a system designed to look for any bits that go 'missing'. If they do, the V.42 hardware will be able to replace them or at least warn the user that some data has gone awry. Most modern modems – certainly the higher performance models – have some sort of error correction built in, so you aren't likely to run into data loss problems.

You should also get a 'Hayes compatible' modem – luckily most modems are. Hayes is a modem manufacturer whose design specifications have become accepted as the industry standard. It developed the 'Hayes command set' which is how computers communicate with the modem. Similarly you should only use a modem that has the official BT green sticker on it. This means that it has been tested by the British Approvals Board for Telecommunications (BABT) and is cleared to be used on the UK's telephone system – any modem that has a red sticker or no sticker at all should be avoided, because if you connect it to a phone line, technically, you are breaking the law.

Tech Box: ISDN and Leased Lines

The standard ISDN service provides two 64000 bps 'B' (Bearer) channels for carrying data and a single 16000 bps 'D' (Delta) channel which looks after the running of the first two and carries information like the number dialled. The service is provided over a standard two-wire phone line that carries the three digital signals. The two B channels can also be combined to provide a 128 kbps link.

As well as the increased bandwidth, ISDN enables you to run separate links allowing a user to send a fax or have a phone conversation while maintaining the data link. Large offices may opt for multiple connections and use up to 30 B channels and a D channel.

Leased lines are dedicated, 24-hours-a-day circuits that your phone company runs directly from your door to your Internet service provider; you can use them to send voice or data between two points. There are several types of leased lines, and they handle data rates from 56 000 bps up to 45 million bps. Often, they are fibre-optic cabling, though they can be copper. At the top of the heap are the most expensive services, T1 and T3 lines, which run at 1.544 million bps and 45 million bps, respectively.

A T1 line is made up of 24 separate channels, each of which can transmit data at a rate of 64 000 bps; there's another 8000 bps channel for signalling and control, which lets you identify the caller's number and track the amount of bandwidth a line is using, among other things. A T3 line is equivalent to 30 T1 lines, providing an overall bandwidth of 45 million bps.

Connecting the Modem to your PC

This item bit gets its own section because a lot of users think that connecting things to computers should be filed under 'Technical'. This is untrue. Thus connecting your modem to your PC is really quite straightforward. There are only a couple of things to look out for and once you have them sorted you should be fine. This section only refers to connecting an external modem – if you have an internal modem (which is an add-in card) you won't have to do any of this. In this case, because you are fiddling with the inside of your computer, you *will* need to follow the instructions that come with the card *very* carefully.

There is likely to be software for your modem with the computer. If there isn't, this is not a problem, but you will need to set up your computer's software so that it recognizes

▽ Tech Box: Watch Out for Older PCs 27

the modem that is connected to it. Microsoft Windows 95 is better than its predecessor (Windows 3.1) at recognizing new hardware, so you should only need to run the 'Add New Hardware' program to connect it, although it is well worth reading the modem's manual first.

It is best to connect the two with your computer and modem switched off. It is possible to connect them with both units on, but you're inviting trouble. Also, you are likely to need to restart your computer once you have installed the software for the modem.

If your modem doesn't come with one, you will need a cable to connect your PC and modem together. The cable plugs into the serial port of the PC, which is either labelled as the −serial− port or, in the new parlance of 'icon language', could be represented by a series of ones and zeros like this 10101 (or have a little logo of a telephone).

The only concern here is the size of the socket. Some PCs have 9 pin sockets others (generally a bit older) 25 pin sockets. Most cables that are supplied with modems are 'multi head', that is, have both a 9 pin and a 25 pin plug at one end − and a single plug that fits into the modem at the other. If you have a problem with this (say, your plug is too small for the socket), it is easy to get a converter, which is simply a piece of plastic with a 9 pin plug at one end and a 25 pin plug at the other.

Tech Box: Watch Out for Older PCs (and their UARTS)

It is likely that with the advent of Windows 95 you will be using a modern PC, but there are some that have older computers or computers that have been upgraded, in which case there is something to watch out for.

The UART (Universal Asynchronous Receiver Transmitter) Chip

The PC uses the UART processor in its serial port to convert the serial data stream from the modem to the PC's internal parallel data system – and vice versa. Alas, the original IBM PC used an 8250 chip as its UART processor and in 1984 the IBM PC AT came out with the 16450. The drawback is they both only collect data one byte at a time, making them reliable only up to speeds of 9600 bps (any faster and they can lose data).

Unfortunately a lot of PCs these days still have these chips running their serial ports, leading to potential data loss at very high speeds. The immediate solution is to replace either your 8250 or 16450 with the much improved 16550 chip which has two 16 byte buffers (one for data coming in and the other for data going out) and will allow your PC to collect data much faster and more reliably.

The only sensible way to do this is to 'replace' your serial port by buying a new serial port add-in card that has a 16550 on it – it simply plugs in to a free slot and replaces your old system. Windows 95 then senses this chip and will use it when necessary. New cards are not expensive.

Internet Browsers

When you arrive at the Internet you need a bit of help seeing what is there. In fact what you need is a piece of software that converts the data your computer is receiving into either pictures or text. This is called a *browser* – a very simple concept as you are actually browsing pages on the Web. Think of it as the Internet's equivalent of 3D glasses – to catch the action you need to be wearing them, otherwise it all looks a bit odd.

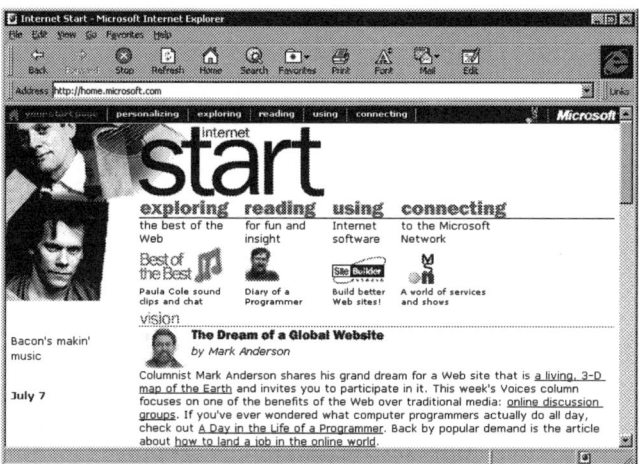

Microsoft's popular Internet Explorer browser

Browsers not only show you the pictures on the Net but they will also give you access to Usenet (Newsgroups) and allow you to have conversations with different people there. They also allow you to view any graphics that are part of the newsgroup message – and enable you to upload images yourself.

Unfortunately browsers come in and out of fashion more than Paris collections, making it 'interesting' for the user – to say the least. In the early days of the Web the most successful browser was Spry Mosaic and this made selection easy. Alas, the problem with the programs available was that they were free – making them very popular – but also unfortunately they were also 'work in progress' and thus not finished. The instant the software was completed the companies would charge for it so users would stick with the unfinished software. Users could get into all sorts of trouble if they downloaded a particularly buggy piece of software.

CHAPTER 3 ▽ What you need to start

(Buggy is computer speak for 'not finished yet' and generally describes programs that don't work fully; often they just stop working, and sometimes even stop the computer working for no apparent reason. Always beware unfinished software.)

Spry is still popular today, but its popularity was very soon overshadowed by Netscape Navigator. In a very short time this became the Next Big Thing and became very popular indeed. Like the software before it, its popularity was helped by Netscape making beta versions available on the Net. Its popularity also helped to push forward the development of the various features that are now standard in a browser and through this time the add-on bits that allowed the different animations and 'twiddly bits' on Web pages were developed.

And then, after the success of Navigator, the big boys joined in the game: Microsoft stepped in with its Internet Explorer program.

Explorer originally came with the Microsoft Windows 95 Plus pack, and as the popularity of the Net grew Microsoft quickly got version 2.0 out. This was quite an unusual thing for Microsoft, because not only did it only make the software available on the Internet, but it also made the finished version free. Before long Microsoft also made early (beta) versions of Internet Explorer 3.0 available on the Net, and, as that was finished, it went on to develop Internet Explorer 4.0 which has a more sophisticated interface. (You may want to check out the latest version of the software by looking at the Microsoft Web site at `http:\\www.microsoft.com\ie\`.)

CHAPTER 4
Your computer hardware – what you need

If talking about the insides of computers make you nervous you might want to take a few deep breaths before you read on. This chapter will tell you the kind of PC you need to surf the Net. If you are thinking of buying a computer to go on line, then give this chapter a browse before you part with any money; and if you are the hardy type and are considering upgrading your current computer, there is information about that too.

The chapter is broken down into sections that cover the different parts of the computer and each section explains what that part of the computer does. But first is 'The Global View', which outlines what you need to start with.

CHAPTER 4 ▽ Your Computer Hardware – What you Need

The Global View

Unfortunately surfing the Net isn't a pastime that uses only one bit of a PC, so we can't advise you to work on your computer's biceps or running technique to make it perform better. You are constrained by the operating system your computer is running. Most people who buy PCs today are going to end up with Microsoft's Windows 95. This has its own needs and you have to satisfy those before you start with any Internet business.

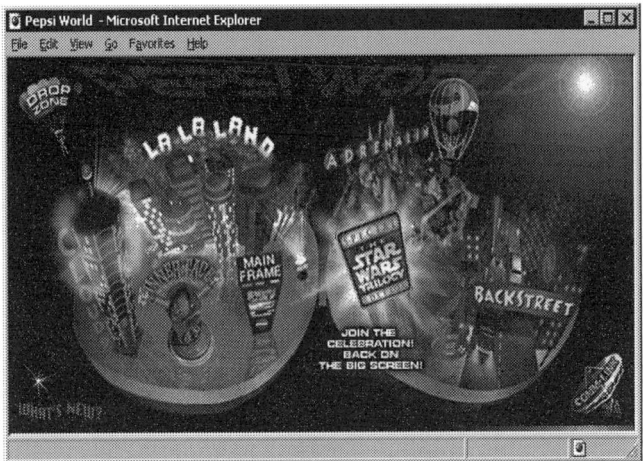

Pepsi's dazzling multimedia site at http://www.pepsi.com/

You will probably have heard of multimedia. It has been a buzzword in the computer world for a while now. In the simplest terms it means 'audio visual' – that is, pictures with sound. It gets a bit more complicated than that when it grows to include multimedia software that enables the user to 'interact' with it. This is when the pictures and sound become part of the 'computer experience'.

The Internet is becoming a multimedia experience. On your journeys you can quite easily come across a sound or video clip

▽ **The Processor**

and you are going to want to be able to hear or see it. There are more and more technologies growing on the net that are going to stretch your PC to its fullest, and to get the best from the Internet your PC needs to be ready for them. Today, many computers are being sold as 'multimedia ready'. To get the most out of the Internet, this is the best route to go, but you mustn't forget you also need to be multimedia ready to get the most out of it.

In this section we shall talk about some of the things that make up a computer and the specifications you need to run Windows 95 and then anything on top of that to make your surfing a bit easier. Don't be discouraged if your computer doesn't have what we recommend, most people can get by with what they have and don't need lots and lots of extra pieces. If you want, you can always have a go at upgrading your current computer instead of buying a new one, although in the long term it is probably best to buy a new computer if you feel your current one doesn't do the job. We should, however, warn you now: too much upgrading can seriously damage your mental health.

The Processor

The processor is the 'brain' of the computer; like the conductor of an orchestra, it sets the pace of the work being done, organizes the work and then does it. There are two factors to bear in mind with the processor: its power and its speed. Its speed (also known as clock speed – from the fact that, like the conductor, it sets the speed of the work to be done) is quite easy to tell as it is part of the name and measured in megahertz or MHz, thus if you see a 66 MHz 486 you'll know that the 66 bit is the speed. The rule of thumb is that the faster the speed the faster the processor runs. Therefore a 33 MHz 486 is slower than a 66 MHz 486.

Judging a processor's power is more difficult, mainly because it doesn't have a simple value to it, but it is still straightforward if you remember the Numbering Rule. What is the Numbering

CHAPTER 4 ▽ Your Computer Hardware – What you Need

Rule? Simply, the bigger the number the more powerful the processor. The first PC processor was called the 8088, the next big thing was the 80286, the one after that the 80386 and the one after that the 80486. Quite simple, huh? You should be getting the hang of this by now.

These were all made by a company called Intel, and Intel, seeing it was onto a good thing, decided it wanted to copyright its processor's name. Unfortunately, it discovered it couldn't copyright numbers, thus it never brought out the 586 (by now it had dropped the leading '80'). Instead it brought out the Pentium processor. Meanwhile, it's worth noting that other companies copied the Pentium – but called their versions the 586.

Now, each of these different processors was a generation improved on the previous one. So if you want a more powerful processor than the 486 you go for a Pentium, if you want a 'more powerful' Pentium you go for a Pentium that has a higher clock speed like, say, 133 MHz or 200 MHz.

The next generation after Pentium is slightly confusingly called Pentium Pro. This processor, along with its sister, the equally-oddly named Pentium II, is more expensive, and carries few gains for the ordinary computer-user.

To run Windows 95 you really need a Pentium and the faster the Pentium the better, although you certainly can get by on a 486, but do not consider buying a 486 PC to run Windows 95 now. If you are buying new, always try to get the most powerful computer you can afford – it is even worth holding back for a few months until you have the right money to buy the right computer.

If you already have a computer and if you have the rest of the correct specifications, a 66 MHz 486 will do to run Windows 95 – but don't expect it to run very fast.

In the early days Internet applications didn't need much processor power, but lately things have changed, Now that we are seeing more graphical 'twiddly' bits (usually small animations) on Web pages, it is more important to have a faster and more powerful processor. Try to get a PC with a 166 MHz or greater Pentium: this gives you some time before it runs out of steam when running your other software, and it will take on everything the Internet can throw at it.

Processor Upgrade

Some computers have a processor that can be replaced by a more powerful processor. There are different types available, but probably the best known is the Intel Overdrive range, replacing 486 and Pentium processors with faster types. Probably the greatest increase is gained with the 486 because it is replaced by the 'next generation up' Pentium processor. This is not to say that there aren't advantages to be had by upgrading a Pentium: the early Pentium processors weren't that much faster than the 486 versions they replaced, and the new Pentium Overdrive processors make a big difference for most applications.

For many computers it is a simple task of unplugging the old processor and plugging in the new one – but for some it's a bit more fiddly, and for others it's impossible.

Intel provide a service to tell you if your computer can be upgraded, and a lot of computer shops and companies will upgrade the computer for you. If you don't want to get your hands dirty, get someone from the shop that sold you your Overdrive to do it for you.

A processor upgrade and extra memory (see below) will certainly breathe new life into your PC and keep it viable for a couple of years, assuming other peripherals are up to the task.

Memory

Also called RAM (Random Access Memory), computer memory is not unlike our own. The computer, like us, will put things in memory that it wants to do now, instead of putting it somewhere more permanent: where we might write it on a bit of paper, a computer uses the hard disk (see Hard Disk, below).

To run Windows 95 you need a minimum of 8 megabytes (or Mb) of memory; to run Windows 95 well, you really need 16, 24 or even 32 Mb. If you're buying a new PC, try to get one with at least 16 Mb RAM, because software in the future is certainly going to want more than we use now). Remember, performance improves as you add more memory.

Playing on the Internet doesn't actually need any extra memory, but like the processor, the more you have the faster the computer runs – more is better. If there is one thing you can do to improve your PC's performance (even above upgrading the processor), it is *add memory*.

Hard Disk

As we said above, if your own memory is like computer memory, a note on a piece of paper is like a hard disk. The computer needs to be able to keep things when it is switched off, and this is what it uses the hard disk for. When the computer is switched on it loads the bits of software from the hard disk to the memory to start it, then as you want it, it loads the different programs that you want to use from the hard disk to the memory, and back again when you have finished.

To run Windows 95 you can get away with 500 or 600 Mb of hard disk space. Just.

But... You will certainly need more in a very short time because Windows 95 programs are getting bigger and bigger and you'll fill up your 600 Mb almost as soon as you take delivery of your PC.

And ... The Internet is full of interesting bits of software and you will almost certainly want to download them. These can be programs to tell you your Horoscope for the next five years or someone's holiday snap of the Sistine Chapel. With a colour holiday snap taking up to half a megabyte you can see that you will soon be running short of space.

You should look for around 1000 Mb, called a gigabyte (Gb). A 1.5 Gb or 2 Gb hard disk should be on your shopping list.

It is worth noting that the Windows 95 Plus pack has with it a disk compression program that squeezes the data on your hard disk to almost half its size, so you can get almost 1 Gb of space from a 600 Mb hard disk. But don't forget that the Free Lunch Rule applies (as in, there ain't no such thing ...), your computer will be slightly slower as it has to squeeze and unsqueeze the data as it comes on and off your hard disk and there is very little chance of recovering your data if it fails. On the other hand, it is a perfect stopgap to tide you over.

Video

This isn't the thing that sits near your TV and records everything but the last five minutes of the film you want to watch, this is the piece of computer hardware that makes the pictures for your PC's monitor to display.

In fact the video card is very important to your system; pictures need processing power. There is a lot of data flowing around the inside of your computer when it's making pictures, so you can improve your computer's performance by getting a faster, or more powerful, video card – alas, the improvement in performance isn't real (inasmuch as your computer is not actually running faster) it is just that the screen responds

CHAPTER 4 ▽ Your Computer Hardware – What you Need

faster – your computer *feels* faster. Which means you spend less time waiting for things to appear – which means you work more quickly (and feel less frustrated), so despite the computer calculations not actually being faster you work quicker.

The Internet is a hard taskmaster for your PC's graphics system, as pictures demand a lot from the hardware that displays it. Unfortunately there is no short cut when it comes to displaying pictures, you need a powerful graphics processor (installed on the graphics card) and video memory (also on the graphics card) to do it.

The deal is the number of colours, versus the size of the picture.

The size or resolution of the picture on the screen is defined by the number of pixels (pixels are the dots that make up the picture) it takes to show it. Therefore, you may see numbers like 640 × 480 which means the picture is made up of 640 pixels across the top of the screen and 480 pixels down the side. The standard picture sizes, in descending order, are 1280 × 1024, 1024 × 768, 800 × 600 and 640 × 480.

Now, to display lots of colours (the colour depth) takes up video memory, so if you want to have lots of colours you compromise on the size of the picture, and if you want a big picture you have fewer colours – or you get more memory. There are four levels of colour supported by normal graphics cards: 16, 256, 65 000 and 16.7 million colours (It may help to know that the Internet is really 256 colours *minimum*).

Most cards start with 1 megabyte of video memory, also called VRAM (Video Random Access Memory). This means if you want to show 256 colours you can display picture sizes up to 1024 × 764, but if you want to show 16.7 million colours you need to go down to 640 × 480. A 2 megabyte video card means you can display 65 000 colours at 1024 × 764 resolution; 4 Mb shifts the numbers up once again.

This may sound complicated, but it has to be remembered that the Web is a graphical environment, and as time progresses the pictures shown there will get bigger with more colours. If you currently have a graphics card with 1 megabyte of VRAM you are OK but you may want to investigate if you can upgrade it to 2 or maybe 4 megabytes – this will make it much faster too.

The most popular resolutions today are 800 × 600 (also called SVGA) and 1024 × 768 for those with a 17 inch monitor. Therefore the ideal graphics card would need at least 2 Mb of VRAM to deliver 65 000 colours at a 1024 × 768 resolution. If you want to move to a higher resolution later on, you are best off looking for a video card that lets you upgrade memory beyond 2 megabytes.

A 15 inch monitor running at 800 × 600 resolution is a minimum requirement for new PCs. If you can afford it, a 17 inch monitor will let you work comfortably at 1024 × 768. Before playing with the video card always check that your monitor can display the higher resolution and colours.

MPEG Video

There is a way of getting moving pictures on the Internet (and in lots of games too): it is done by compressing the pictures a particular way, which is generally called MPEG compression. To uncompress and watch the pictures you need a card that supports this, not surprisingly called an MPEG card.

There are a growing number of applications on the web that take advantage of MPEG and it is certainly an advantage to have one. But it is important to note that it is not necessary to have an MPEG card to surf, it is only a useful luxury.

CHAPTER 4 ▽ Your Computer Hardware – What you Need

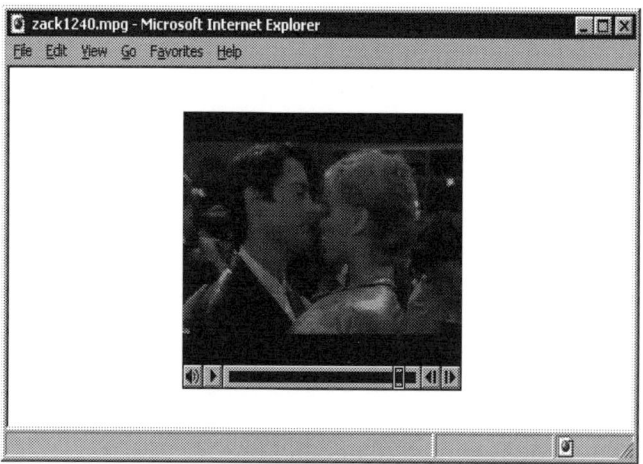

Without an MPEG card, movies are small, but still easily watchable

It is also worth noting that some graphics cards allow you to buy a small add-on card (called a daughter board) that will give your computer MPEG ability. If you are upgrading your video then it is worth investigating this as an option to buy the graphics card now and perhaps upgrade it later (it is even worth checking if your current card can be upgraded).

We shall be seeing MPEG encoded software more and more in the future, so it may well be worth investigating it sooner rather than later.

Monitor

As we have seen that Windows 95 is graphical (or made up of pictures), the monitor you use is now more important that it used to be; this is doubly so now that you are surfing the Web which is based around pictures.

If you can get a monitor that's larger than the standard 14 inches, do so. Certainly 14 inches should be the absolute minimum for Windows 95. The smaller the monitor, the more likely it is you'll get eyestrain.

A 15 or 17 inch monitor with a 'dot pitch' of 0.28 mm or less is really what you want (the dot pitch is the distance between the little dots that makes up the picture on the screen – the smaller the distance, the sharper the screen image).

Audio

Most PCs now come equipped with some sort of audio capability which makes it simple to pick up most of the sound that is available on the Internet. Anything from using the Net to call people across the world for the price of a local call to listening to Internet radio.

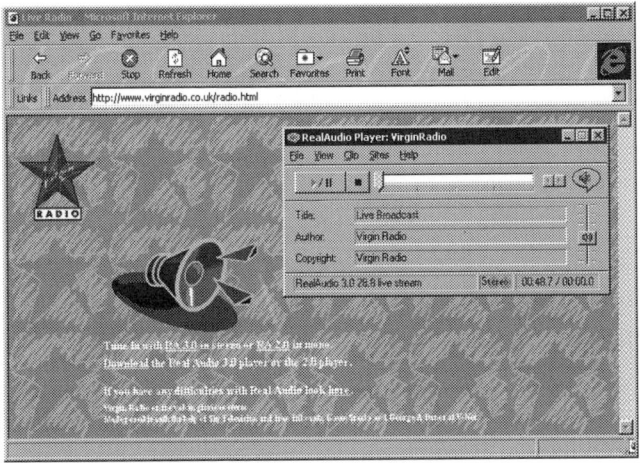

Listen to Virgin Radio Live on the Net at http://www.virginradio.co.uk/radio.html

All the same, some computers still need to be upgraded and that means buying a sound card of some description. Look for a more versatile sound card that can be used for games and even making music, so you should be aiming for a card that will support the General MIDI (Musical Instrument Digital Interface), GM, standard. MIDI is a standard set of commands that can be issued by an electronic instrument (more than likely, a keyboard) or an application (probably a game). Since a MIDI command demands less storage than digitized sound files, it is prevalent in game and edutainment titles.

For business users a card that combines sound functionality with communications functions is useful. With special chips called DSPs (digital signal processors), these combination cards provide basic PC sound while adding things like fax, and voice mail. The newer cards even have voice recognition and the ability to convert text to speech, so you can control your computer with voice commands and print out what you say.

Most sound cards have a built-in amplifier, but the volume isn't very high. Better sound systems need speakers that have an amplifier built in. These are more expensive, but will sound clearer.

Still Worried?

There are some good and interesting products you can get for your computer, but it means rummaging inside your PC. If this is a problem look for a computer supplier that will install the card and set your PC up for you - they aren't difficult to find and shopping around will also get you a good price.

CHAPTER 5
How does the software work?

We'll be introducing you to how to use the Internet in later chapters, but first of all it's useful to see what the software looks like.

Anatomy of a Browser

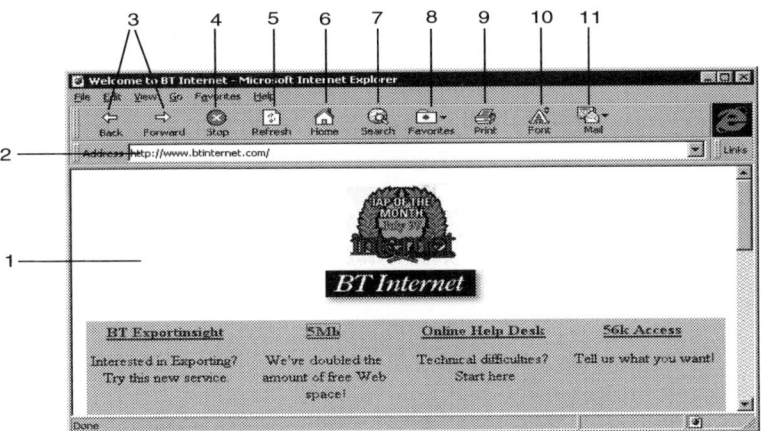

CHAPTER 5 ▽ How does the software work?

1. *The main window.* The Web pages you view are shown here.
2. *The address.* Also known as the Uniform Resource Locator (URL); this is where the page you are viewing is actually located. It consists of the name of a computer somewhere, and the location of the page on that computer's disk.
3. *Backwards and forwards buttons.* If you follow a link on a Web page and you want to go back again, click the Back button and the previous page reappears. Click the Forward button and you'll be back to where you were.
4. *Stop.* If a page is loading very slowly, but you can already see the information you're interested in, click this button and your browser will stop trying to download the rest of the page and let you get on with browsing.
5. *Refresh.* If you want to start reloading a page from scratch, click Refresh. If a page seems to have stopped downloading, it's worth clicking this button to see if you can get the process going again.
6. *Home.* The 'home page' is the first page your browser displays when you start it (You can change this page from the 'View, Options' menu, mentioned below.) Clicking the Home button will return you to this page at any time during your browsing.
7. *Search.* Jumps to a page of search engines (more on those in Chapter 9) where you can search for information on a particular subject.
8. *Favorites.* If you want to keep track of your favourite Web pages, you can save shortcuts to them here and return to them anytime with just a couple of clicks. To add the page your currently viewing, click this button, then click Add to Favorites. To return to a page you've stored in this way, click the Favorites button and select the name of the page from the list.
9. *Print.* As you'd expect, if you click this button, the page you're looking at will be printed out on paper.
10. *Font.* Click here repeatedly to move through different text sizes or, for easier control, click the View menu and go to Fonts.
11. *Mail.* Open a short menu from which you can start your e-mail or newsreader programs, send someone an e-mail

Anatomy of a News Reader

message, or send them a link to the web page you're looking at.

Many of the functions above are duplicated on Internet Explorer's menus. The menus do hold some useful bits and pieces though. The file menu allows you to save the current page either in its original HTML format (so that you can look at it later in your browser) or as a text file so that you can look at it in a text editor. The View menu lets you turn the toolbars on and off to gain more viewing area, and leads to the Options set of tabbed pages where you can customize the browser to your own taste.

Anatomy of a News Reader

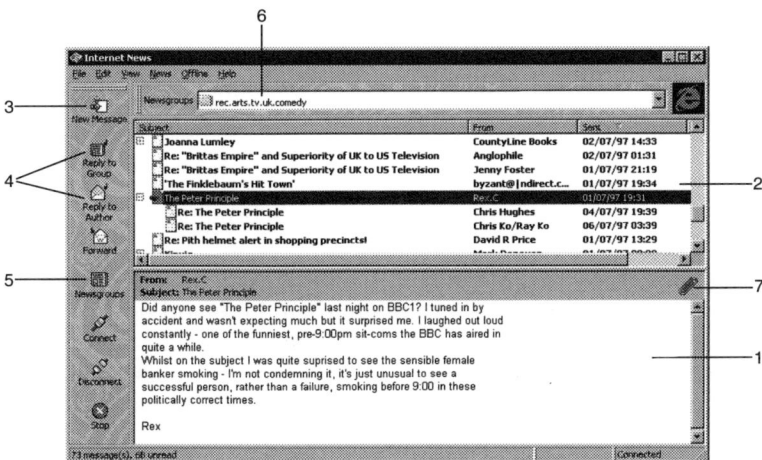

1. *Message window*: This shows the content of the current message. To see which one it is, look at the list of headers, and see which one is highlighted.
2. *Headers*: Shows the subjects of the messages you have downloaded, who sent them, when they were received, and

CHAPTER 5 ▽ How does the software work?

how long the message is. Note that lots are marked with 'Re:'. That shows they are a reply to an earlier message.
3. *New message*: Got a burning question on your mind? Click this to compile a message for the newsgroup.
4. *Reply to group/author*: Will send your comments on the message in the current window. One will post to the newsgroup, one by e-mail. When do you use each one? You'll have to read Chapter 7 to find out.
5. *Newsgroups*: Finds the list of newsgroups and helps you to search it.
6. *Current newsgroup*: That's where you are now. Hit the down arrow on the right of the box to see a list of recently-visited newsgroups, and click on the name to revisit one of them.
7. *File attachment*: Click on the paper clip to see the encoded file that was sent with this message; on Usenet, this is almost always a picture file – either called 'filename.gif' or 'filename.jpg'. You'll see the paper clip in Microsoft browsers, and browsers that are related to it. Netscape browsers automatically display the picture in the message window instead.

Anatomy of an E-mail Reader

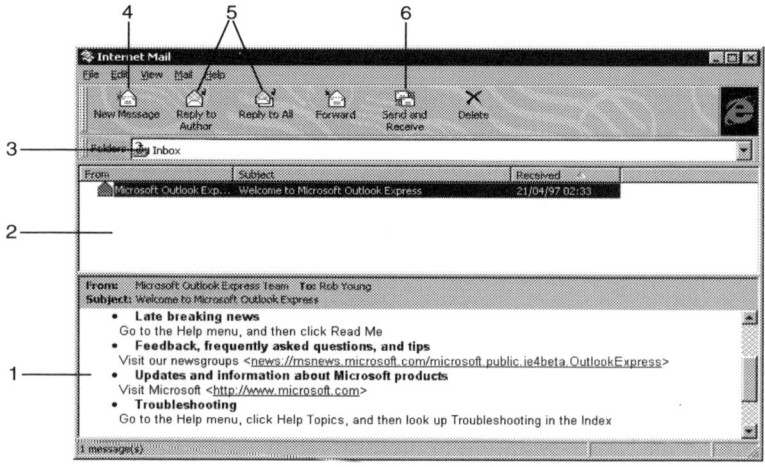

Anatomy of an E-mail Reader

1. *Message window*: The contents of the selected message.
2. *List of messages*: In this case we're in the inbox, so this is a list of messages received. If we were in the outbox, it would be a list of messages that we had sent. It shows the subject, and the date. Replies to messages are automatically named 'Re: [message title]'.
3. *Inbox or outbox?* Select it here. Also shows the messages you have deleted.
4. *New message*: Want to send some mail? Click this button, and you'll get a form to fill in. To find out how to send mail, see Chapter 6.
5. *Reply to Author/Reply to All*: Click this to send a reply. 'Reply to Author' means just to the person who sent you the message. 'Reply to All' means the message will go to all the other people who received this message too – be careful, a mistake could be very embarrassing. There's the true story of the woman who tried to send a nude picture of herself to her boyfriend, and sent it to her entire company instead . . .
6. *Send and receive*: If you have composed all your messages offline (i.e. not connected to the Internet), hit this button and your mail reader will dial up the Internet, post all your new messages and retrieve all your incoming mail.

CHAPTER 6

It's in the post

E-mail is one of the great bargains of the Internet. Sending messages is almost instant, to anywhere in the world. You can e-mail anyone else on the Net, from Bill Gates (billg@microsoft.com) to your next door neighbour. Because mail is quick, it doesn't take much phone time; you can prepare the message, then dial up, send and receive your mail and hang up in less than a minute.

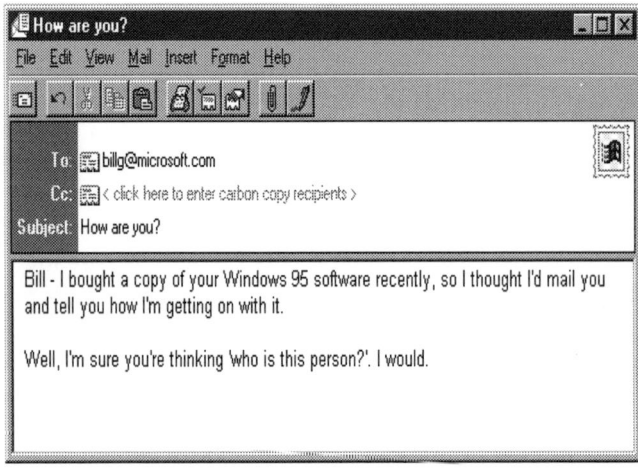

How Do I Send Mail?

It couldn't be easier. When you tell your mail reader that you want to send a message, it pops up a form for you to fill in. You tell it who the message goes to by typing the recipient's e-mail address in the 'To:' box. You tell it if you want anyone else to get a carbon copy by using the 'cc:' box (that is in case you ever wondered what ' cc:' stands for), and you give the message a title.

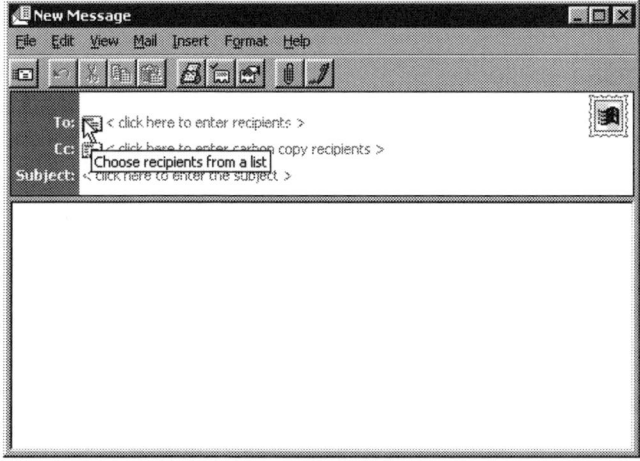

Click the little card symbol beside the 'To' and 'CC' lines to choose recipients from your Address Book list

Then click in the message box, and type the text. When you are finished, hit ' Send message', and off it goes! If you are already on line, you probably won't notice anything. If you are not on line, your computer will need to dial up the Internet first.

That's really as hard as it gets. When you reply to a message, the recipient and the subject are automatically filled in for you, so it's even easier than starting a conversation.

CHAPTER 6 ▽ It's in the post

Don't forget to sign your e-mails, so that the recipient knows what your real name is. Don't assume they will guess – it's embarrassing for both parties if they send back a message saying 'Who are you?'.

What Does an E-mail Address Mean?

E-mail addresses are quite remarkable things if you think about it. In one funny line of text is an address that is unique to you, and will find you anywhere in the world. An address is broken down like this:

```
|1        |2   |3          |4|
yourname@company.domain.co.uk
```

1. The first part is your user name: it can be anything you want, but most people use either their full name (timphillips) or an initial plus last name (tphillips) or a first name plus initial of last name (timp). There's no hard and fast rule.
2. The '@' sign says that this person is connected to a certain computer. It's like the difference between your name and your address on an envelope.
3. Anything after the @ sign defines a computer or a network of computers. Usually there will be the name of a company (if it's a work address) or the name of a service provider (like BTInternet). That is what the 'domain' is.
4. The last bit tells you where the computer or network is situated, and what that organization does. 'co.uk' means a commercial organization based in the UK. '.com' means an international commercial organization. '.org' means a non-profit commercial organization. Here's a list of some of the most common:

   ac   academic institution (university, usually; it's how you spot a student)

▽ Where Do I Find Someone's E-mail Address? 51

gov	government
net	Internet administrative host
uk	United Kingdom
fr	France
aus	Australia
de	Germany
jp	Japan

Why are there no ' co.us' addresses?, you ask. That's because the Americans invented this system when the Internet wasn't international, so they are all '.com'. There are some new types of name popping up all the time: 'uk.com' has been sighted too. When you joined the service you will have been given your e-mail address. That's your new name.

Where Do I Find Someone's E-mail Address?

You could guess, but if you get one character wrong, even a lower-case letter when it is meant to be a capital letter, your message will 'bounce' straight back to you with an attached message to say ' user unknown'. That's Internet for ' return to sender'. So it's usually easier to look it up.

There's no central database of e-mail addresses or an e-mail phone book, but there are some services which do a similar job:

Bigfoot
http://www.bigfoot.com
Claims that more than a million people have registered. You visit the site, look for the address you want, and leave your own details for others to find.

CHAPTER 6 ▽ It's in the post

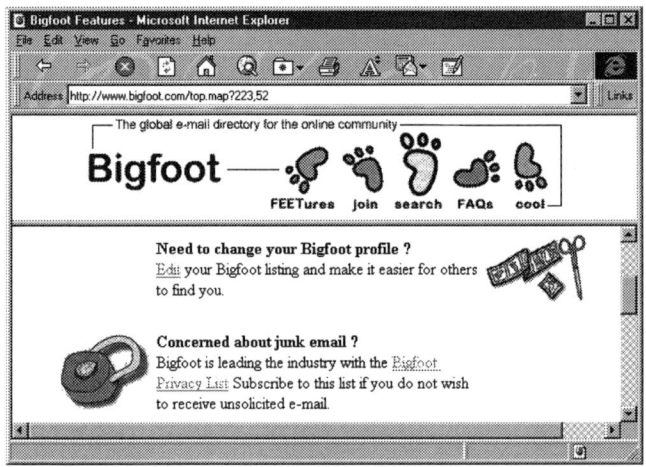

Looking for someone's e-mail address? Bigfoot is a large step in the right direction

Deja News
http://www.dejanews.com
Really a service to let you search Usenet, but when you post to Usenet, your e-mail address is captured too. So if the person you are looking for has posted to a newsgroup, search for their name here.

LookUp
http://www.lookup.com

Four11
http://www.four11.com

Often companies allow you to mail from their Web pages too. This rarely puts you in touch with one person, but instead goes through to the site administrator, who forwards the messages as necessary.

E-mail Someone you Don't Know

E-mail also allows you to contact the great and the good. And the bad. And, presumably, the ugly, although on the Internet, you can't tell. Try these well-known people though: but be warned, famous people get hundreds of unsolicited e-mails every day. Few of them reply personally. Usually the best you can hope for is a reply from a flunky or an automated response. Try these:

```
Douglas Adams: 76206.2507@compuserve.com
Paddy Ashdown: paddyashdown@cix.co.uk
Beavis and Butthead: beavis@mtv.com. butthead@mtv.com
Tom Clancy: tomclancy@aol.com
Bill Clinton: President@WhiteHouse.gov
Bill Gates: billg@microsoft.com
John Grisham: 71035.1742@compuserve.com
Charles Grodin: CharlesGrodin@aol.com
Bob Hoskins: 75300.1313@compuserve.com
Billy Idol: idol@phantom.com
Garrison Keillor: gkeillor@madmax.mpr.org
Ross Perot: 71511.460@compuserve.com
Terry Pratchett: tpratchett@cix.co.uk
Santa Claus: santa@north.pole.org
```

CHAPTER 7
Usenet – the Internet speakeasy

All the news that's fit to print, and a lot that isn't, is found in the 25 000 or so Usenet newsgroups. This is the internet in its purest form: people from all over the world saying what they want, leaving messages about anything they want. Usenet can be the most useful part of the Internet if you want to meet other people. It is also bandit country: the shock-horror tales of bomb-making, pornography and abuse that you read about in the tabloids usually originate here.

Still interested? Let's explain what usenet is.

Newsgroups

Usenet is a text-only service organized into groups, called newsgroups. Few of them actually contain news: 'opinionsgroups' would be a better description, though harder to pronounce. Instead, you can contribute to the discussion and debate in any newsgroup, just by typing a message. Usenet relies on Internet users – it's like a huge pub. And like the pub, there are bores and rude drunks as well as your mates.

There are thousands of newsgroups, some of which have hundreds of new messages a day, some of which haven't been active for weeks. Each group contains discussion on a relatively narrow topic. Let's take an imaginary example – rec.bananas.peeled.

Not a user-friendly name is it? Usenet newsgroups get more specific from left to right, so 'rec' stands for ' recreational'. There are other categories – ' uk' for British subjects is one category to look for. Next is the main subject (bananas), then a subcategory (peeled). There might also be a subcategory for people who want to discuss rec.bananas.unpeeled.

At the time of writing, these newsgroups don't exist, but at the rate the Internet is growing, we expect a wired banana enthusiast will start one soon. If you want to discuss peeled bananas, it's very bad form to discuss it in rec.football. It is also very bad form to discuss peeled bananas in rec.bananas.unpeeled. Your fellow Net users will remind you curtly that you have breached Netiquette (see Chapter 14 for a Netiquette primer).

Usenet Discussion

To give this anarchy some structure, Usenet discussions are divided into ' says' and 'comments'. If you want to start a new discussion, you 'say'. Other people who want to comment on what you said, 'comment'. You can comment on comments, until everyone has exhausted the subject. This is called a 'thread'. Every newsgroup has many threads running at any one time. You can comment to any thread. We'll show you how to do this later in the chapter.

CHAPTER 7 ▽ Usenet – the Internet speakeasy

Here's the hard bit: your messages may end up in several newsgroups. If there were a newsgroup called `rec.bananas`, it would contain everything in `rec.bananas.peeled`, and `rec.bananas.unpeeled`. If you post to `rec.bananas.peeled`, your message will pop up in `rec.bananas` too.

This seems perverse, but it is very sensible. If you have a broad interest in bananas, then you can read a lot of general messages in `rec.bananas`. If you have a narrow interest in peeled bananas but unpeeled bananas bore you, read fewer messages in `rec.bananas.peeled`.

How Does Usenet Work?

Without getting too complicated, your service provider has a 'news server' which contains the last few days' messages on Usenet. From time to time, other news servers connect to it, and they swap new messages. This process goes on all over the world on every news server, and your message is spread slowly from server to server over a matter of hours or days. This means that other users may not be replying to your message yet because they haven't received it. Although you can see it on your server, they can't see it on theirs.

Posting a Message

To go to any newsgroup, you simply type in its URL. For Web sites this begins with HTTP. For newsgroups, it logically begins with NEWS.

Log on and fire up your Web browser. When you are on line, type

    news:alt.test

▽ Posting a Message

in the 'Location' box, and after a little while the newsgroup dedicated to test messages for your connection pops up. In

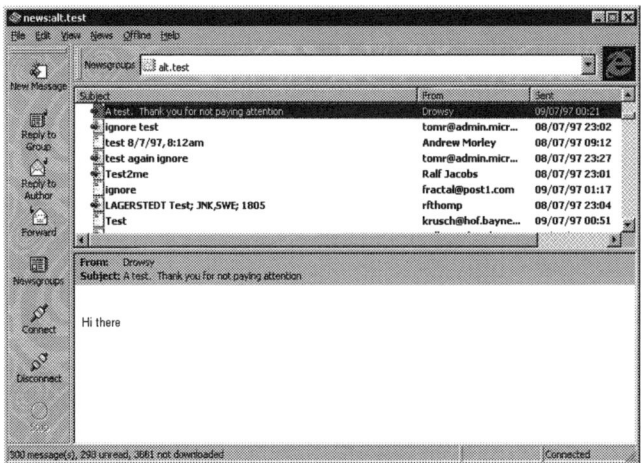

alt.test is the perfect group for beginners and anyone trying out a different news program for the first time

the top window are the message headers; in the bottom window the message contents.

You may be surprised to notice that as well as test messages, the newsgroup contains replies from people who are experienced users. The Internet sometimes does this to people. Previously quite normal, they become compulsive communicators, and reply to messages like 'testing testing'.

We're going to send a message with the content 'testing testing' to see if we get any replies.

Click on 'New Message'. It's the first button. The message window inserts the newsgroup you are browsing in the 'Newsgroups:' line. You can add more group names by typing them on the line separating names by a space. Don't do it this time.

CHAPTER 7 ▽ **Usenet – the Internet speakeasy**

Then enter the subject. This is what comes up in the 'subject' line. Type 'testing', or whatever.

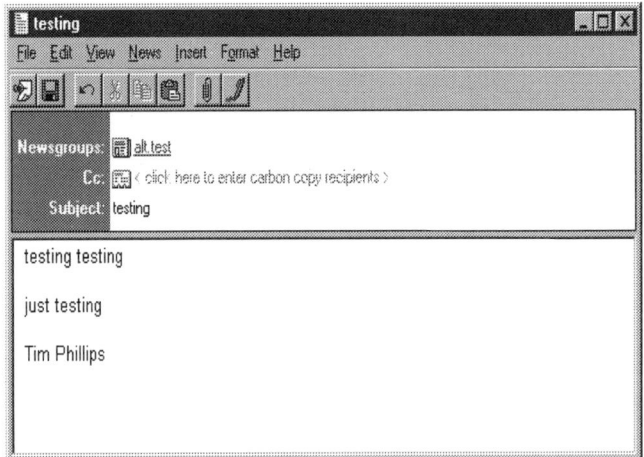

Your new message to alt.test will look something like this

Finally, type a message in the message window, and post. You'll see the message straight away, but it will take time to reach the rest of the world.

Responding to Other Messages

Commenting is just as simple; although you have the choice of 'Reply to Group' or 'Reply to Author'. One posts to the newsgroup; one sends e-mail. The difference is that e-mail is private to that user and gets there immediately; if you want, it's fine to do both.

Find a test message from someone else, hit 'Reply to Group', and you find the subject is already inserted. It will be the title of the message you are commenting to with a 'Re:' (for 'reference') on the front. That helps people identify what you are talking about, so leave it.

Type your message, off it goes. Let's not send this response as e-mail, because even new users don't care for messages from strangers that say 'testing testing 123 iwedi2dhwuf'.

Exploring Usenet

Let's find out what else is there. Hit the 'Newsgroups' button (you also get here by selecting 'Read News' from the 'Go' menu of any Web browser). If this is your first visit, you will be asked whether you want to download the list of newsgroups your service provider offers. Agree, and a few minutes later it is time to look around.

If you use a browser based on Microsoft's Internet Explorer, you see a box listing all the newsgroups. Type a subject you like, such as 'films', and the list narrows down to newsgroups which contain the word. Click on the group, then click on 'visit' to go there.

Other browsers allow you to explore the list for scrolling and searching.

You can click on 'Subscribe', which means that whenever you visit news, the headers of the new messages in that group are downloaded to you automatically. This is only useful if you'll keep visiting the group. If in doubt, visit first for a look round.

Usenet may be text-only, but there are many newsgroups that contain pictures that have been posted by being converted to a text-based code, which is posted as a message. Your reader will automatically pick this up. For example, any newsgroup that starts `alt.binaries` is for these pictures.

CHAPTER 7 ▽ Usenet – the Internet speakeasy

Visit an `alt.binaries` newsgroup and click on a long message. If you are using Netscape, the picture will begin to appear in the message window. If you are using a Microsoft browser, a picture of a paper clip will pop up on the right of the message window title bar. Click on the paper-clip and a little menu will appear containing the file or files sent with the message. Click a filename and the picture will be shown.

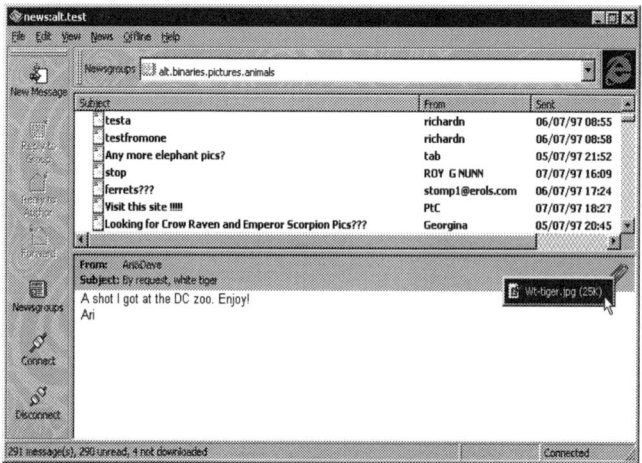

Click on the paper-clip, click the filename, and you'll see the attached picture

It's Not for the Nervous

A warning: Usenet is dedicated to free speech. People can occasionally be rude or insulting. The pornographic pictures can be extreme. Newsgroup discussion can be swamped by petty arguments or tedious waffle. Remember, there's no boss on the Internet. You can criticize the senders, but no one will step in to restore order. You just have to wait a few days!

Some Newsgroups to get you Started

Try these if you don't know where to start. You may have 25 000 to choose from, so if you don't find anything in this list, go and explore.

Computing

`news.newusers.questions`	What this book didn't tell you
`alt.culture.newsnet`	Etiquette for newsgroups
`alt.culture.www`	Using the Web
`alt.comp.shareware`	Shareware chat
`alt.comp.virus`	Discussion – you won't get one
`alt.folklore.computers`	Not all true
`comp.ai`	Artificial intelligence
`comp.answers`	Moderated, but with useful articles
`comp.os.ms-windows`	Windows for everyone

Hobbies

`alt.aquaria`	Sounds fishy
`rec.birds`	Birdwatching
`rec.boats`	Boatwatching
`rec.climbing`	Techniques, competitions
`rec.collecting`	General collector's forum
`rec.crafts`	Life is what you make of it
`rec.fitness`	Work that body on Usenet
`rec.games.chess.misc`	Work that mind on Usenet
`rec.gardens`	Green fingered chat
`rec.martial-arts`	All types
`rec.music.misc`	For music lovers

CHAPTER 7 ▽ Usenet – the Internet speakeasy

Sport

rec.sport.soccer	Named by Americans
uk.sport.athletics	British running, throwing, jumping
alt.flame.sports-suck	If you hate sport
alt.sport.darts	Keeps you out of the pub
alt.tv.sports	For couch potatoes
rec.gambling.sports	Punters only
rec.sport.baseball	You might call it rounders
rec.sport.golf	Keep a six off your card
rec.sport.rugby.league	13 men
rec.sport.rugby.union	15 men
rec.sport.tennis	Racket news and opinions

UK-Specific

uk.media	Magazines, TV, radio, newspapers
alt.politics.british	Some good debate here
soc.culture.british	All about us
alt.music.uk	What do the Americans think of our bands?
alt.radio.uk	Like it says
rec.arts.tv.uk.coronation.st	How British can you get?
uk.announce	General announcements
uk.education.misc	Discussion of education standards
uk.environment	Save the planet – UK first
uk.rec.competitions	Announcements, tips. Join and win
uk.singles	British lonely hearts chat

Trivial but Amusing

alt.music.lyrics	What is that guy singing? Ask here

Some Newsgroups to get you Started

```
rec.food.recipes              Yum
rec.arts.startrek.fandom      Of course
rec.games.trivia              Trivia games
alt.fan.letterman             US talk show host and his
                              'Top 10' lists
```

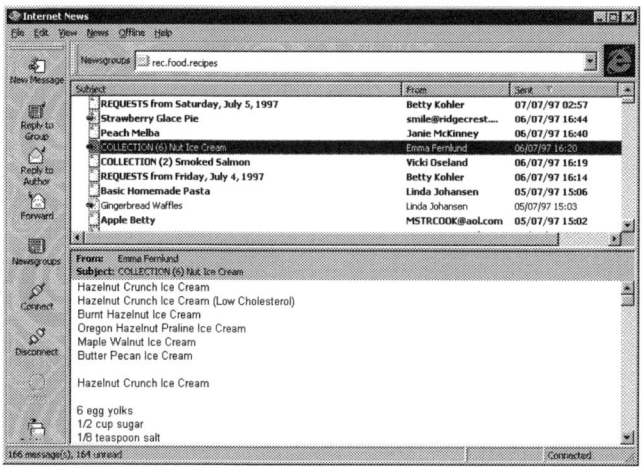

Fancy a free cookbook containing thousands of original recipes? Drop in at rec.food.recipes

Business

```
uk.jobs.offered               If you're looking for work, try
                              here
alt.business.misc             General discussion
alt.business.home.pc          Put that computer to work
```

Jokes, Japes, Funny Business

```
alt.shenanigans               Practical jokes
aus.jokes                     Australian, er, humour
rec.humor                     Some funny, some tasteless
```

CHAPTER 7 ▽ Usenet – the Internet speakeasy

```
rec.humor.funny              Moderated newsgroup – less
                             offensive!
alt.fan.vic-reeves           We wouldn't let it lie
```

Images

```
alt.binaries.clip-art        Useful pictures for
                             documents
alt.binaries.drwho           Monsters. Scary!
alt.binaries.fonts           For alternative types
alt.binaries.pictures        Overall newsgroup for
                             photos
alt.binaries.pictures.utilities  Software to help with your
                             graphics
alt.binaries.sounds.tv       OK, sounds not pictures –
                             but fun
```

CHAPTER 8

Getting caught in the Web

Now let's get to the meat and potatoes: the World Wide Web. Chances are, it's the Web that got you interested in the Internet in the first place.

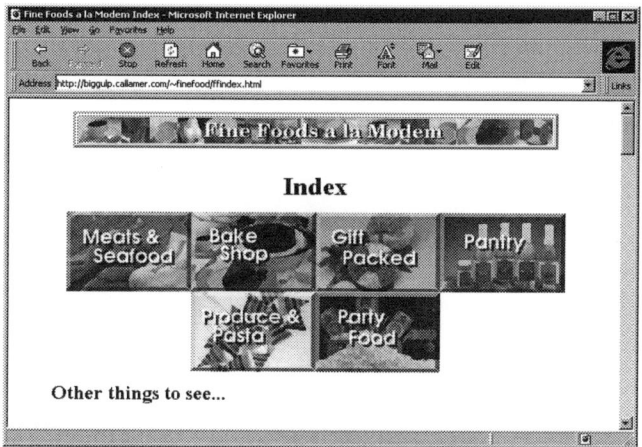

The meat and potatoes, and a lot more too, at
http://biggulp.callamer.com/~finefood/ffindex.html

CHAPTER 8 ▽ Getting caught in the Web

The joy of the Web is that it's easy to explore. Unlike Usenet, or IRC, which can be confusing at first, the words-and-pictures format of the Web make it as easy as browsing a rack of magazines.

For the most part, browsing the Web is a passive activity. You open a page, read what's on it, go to another, read that, and so on until the phone bill arrives. No one is watching, and you don't have to pass any exams first. The main challenge is to your will to explore, which is often why kids like it so much.

Finding your way onto the Web is made easier because, when you start your browser, it opens a 'home page'. This is its default page, which you can set to be your own page, but let's not get ahead of ourselves. First, let's explore a Web site.

We're Off

Fire up your browser, and in the URL box type

    http://www.microsoft.com

and hit enter. That's right, we're visiting Microsoft home page, its office on the Web. Watch the bottom left of the browser window and you will see 'web site found', and some little figures that keep changing. That's the files on the Web page being transferred to your computer.

Give the page a minute to come up. You will see something like this:

▽ **We're Off**

The starting point for Microsoft news, support, software, and free stuff

The page changes regularly – most Web pages do – but you should see something broadly similar.

Does this remind you of anything? It's like a cross between a magazine and a cartoon. Watch closely and you will see that some parts of the screen are moving – small animation programs that your computer downloads with the Web page are doing that. You will also see a big image with options to visit other pages. This is like a contents page. Most Web sites start on a page like this – it is known as the site's 'home page'.

Run your mouse pointer backwards and forwards over the page. Every so often it turns into a little hand. The hand means the pointer is active – that is, if you click the mouse button now, you will go to the page described by the link your pointer is on.

CHAPTER 8 ▽ Getting caught in the Web

When the pointer moves over a link, you'll see it change into a hand

Near the bottom of the page, the same links are written as underlined small text. If you can't wait for the image to download (or have switched image downloading off in your browser, which makes the Web faster to use), these links do the same thing. Generally, any words you see underlined on a Web page will jump to another page if you put your mouse pointer over that word and click.

Look to the far right of the browser window and you will see a grey scroll bar. Web pages don't have to be any particular shape, unlike TV programmes or newspapers, so if you can't see what you want, scroll down the page.

How Do I Browse?

That's a little like asking, 'How do I shop?' The best way is just to click on any link that interests you. If you were wrong, click on the back arrow in your browser to return to where you were before. To go to a completely different site, type its

▽ How Do I Browse?

URL in the Address box, hit return and you're there; although most sites have links to other sites too. For example, if you are browsing a business site, there will normally be a number of links to similar resources. Using nothing but a few mouse clicks, you will often be able to browse for hours.

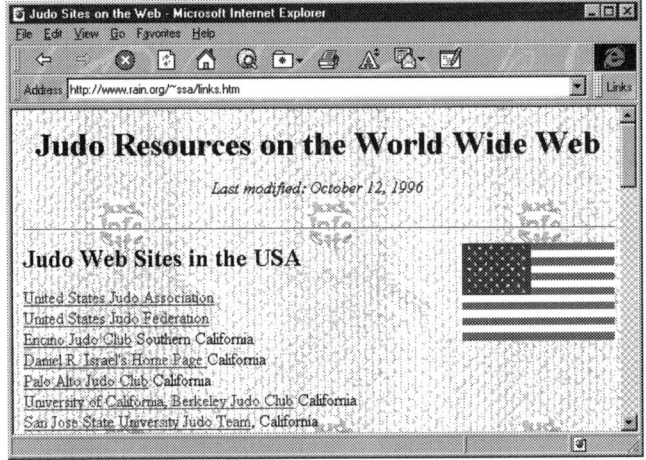

Most pages on the Web provide links to other sites you might find interesting

The time taken to learn how to browse is the time it takes you to click on your first link.

Occasionally you will find a site that asks you to register – that is, to fill in a form telling the user who you are and where you live. It then gives you a nickname and password. Make a note of it.

Registration forms are a pain, but they tell the person who designs the site about the people who visit it. There's nothing sinister about registering – most Web sites have assurances that your information (such as it is) will not be passed on.

CHAPTER 8 ▽ Getting caught in the Web

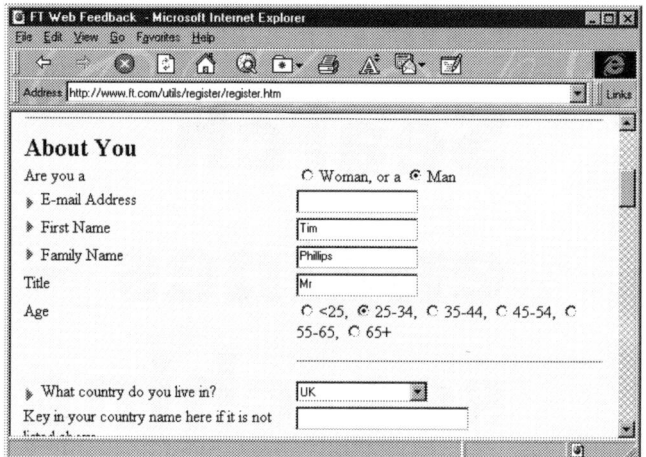

The Financial Times site (http://www.ft.com), among others, asks you to fill in a few details about yourself when you arrive

Some sites charge for entry. To get into these you will need to enter a credit card number; this can be insecure, so be careful. The problems with payment on the Web are dealt with in Chapter 15.

The next two chapters cover more than a hundred of the best sites on the Web. Stop reading about it, and explore.

CHAPTER 9
Search engines – searching for places to go

Once you have got on the Web and have got bored with looking at the sites that are programmed into your browser, you may want to go further afield and look at some others – this is where the search engine becomes very useful.

It's like being in a giant toy shop when you know there are lots of toys you want to look at, but you don't have time to look through each aisle. So you need a helper who knows where everything is, so on a whim you say, 'train sets' and your helper takes you to train sets - and the fun starts.

CHAPTER 9 ▽ Search engines

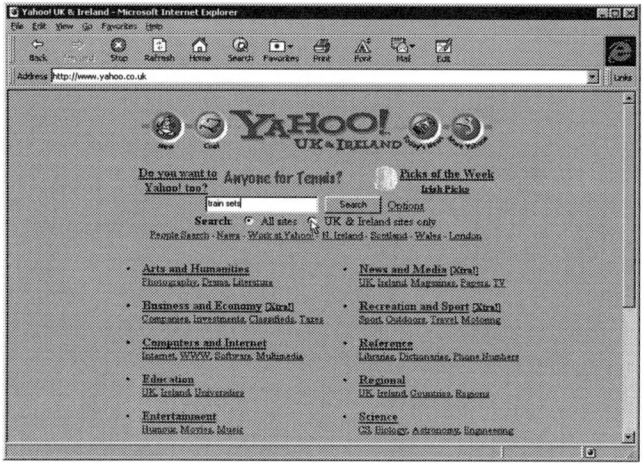

Search for UK or world sites at Yahoo UK & Ireland (http://www.yahoo.co.uk)

It isn't as though you are on your own: a lot of the pages you have been looking at already have a link to some sort of helper or search engine. And if that fails most browsers have search engine addresses written into them, so it is unlikely you will ever be left without any access to these devices.

Search engines are a very simple concept: people who create pages on the web register their new page with a particular search engine, other people go to the search engine and do a search on a particular subject and if that is what this particular site is about the engine throws up the address.

Each search engine page has a search word window where you type the one or two words that describes what you want. Finding the right word can be a little tricky sometimes so it is well worth being patient and thinking laterally if your first attempts aren't getting what you want. For example, if you want to find sites that have humorous cartoon drawings, you are likely to get some if you type 'humour' in the search window, but you will also get all the other humour sites that don't have cartoons. If you type 'cartoons' you will probably get some of the sites you want, but also animated cartoons.

▽ **Search engines**

Some sites allow you to re-sort what they have thrown up so you can do 'cartoons' first then 'humorous'. Of course you may want to search first with two words: 'humorous cartoons'.

Punctuation and the order of the words are generally ignored, so 'cartoons humorous' is equivalent to 'cartoons, humorous' and to 'humorous cartoons'. Quotation marks can turn several words into one term, so the query "humorous cartoons" would lead you only to sites where the words appeared next to each other. This approach is best for searching for names thus "Tony Blair" would throw up matches on the name rather than the words 'Tony' and 'Blair' appearing somewhere in the title.

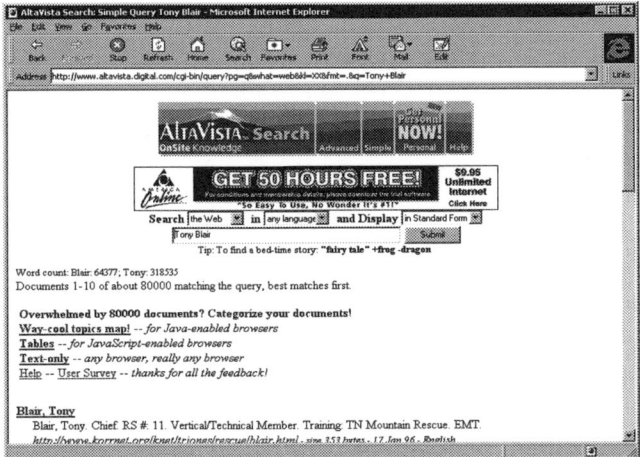

Roughly eighty thousand pages matching "Tony Blair" at AltaVista (http://www.altavista.digital.com)

There are three basic categories of search engine: engines that provide an index to the Web and attempt to index key words on important sites. Here, you enter a word or phrase, and the search engine returns a list of every page that contains a match. After that there are engines that provide categories to search within; these sites serve almost as a

CHAPTER 9 ▽ Search engines

'contents page' to the Web. You can still do key word searches but these search engines have specific areas to search within as well, so you can search under 'sport' or 'business' or 'TV'.

Yahoo, for example, has 14 categories to choose from, including Arts, Business and Economy, News, Science and Recreation and Sports. You can put a search in for anything you like and the search engine will look at the Internet and come up with suggestions. For example if you type in 'spam' you get . . . well, try it yourself and see what you get!

There are also review-based search engines, these do all of the above, but then give you their opinion of what is a good (or 'cool') site. This is all very well if you agree with the ratings they give, if not . . .

Here is a list of search engines that will help you around the Web. First, five engines that, if you don't use any other, will get most of the sites that you'll want:

Yahoo! UK & Ireland
http://www.yahoo.co.UK/
The largest search engine on the web: if you can't find it here it may not exist. Subjects are arranged by category, like a huge library. You can go deeper and deeper into the search system by selecting a sub section under each of the 14 different search areas, so you can look for 'Vogue' under 'Entertainment' and the subsection 'Magazines'.

AltaVista
http://www.altavista.digital.com/
If not the best, it's in the top two of search engines. This will even search newsgroups. It searches for content, so you can enter 'Alas poor Yorick I knew him Horatio' to find the text of *Hamlet* (try it).

Electric Library
http://www.elibrary.com/
Searches online magazines and newspapers.

▽ **Search engines**

Lycos
http://lycos.com
Another heavy duty search engine. As well as key word searches, you can find the Top 5% of sites, search for People, or Pictures and Sounds, or share prices, just by clicking the appropriate buttons. Or narrow down you search by choosing from 18 categories including News, Kids, Fashion and Entertainment.

Magellan
http://mckinley.netcom.com/
Along with the usual key word search facility, Magellan lets you choose from 15 subject categories.

A2Z
http://a2z.lycos.com/
A2Z will search like other engines, but also gives lists of the most frequently-visited sites, leading you to some of the best sites in your chosen category.

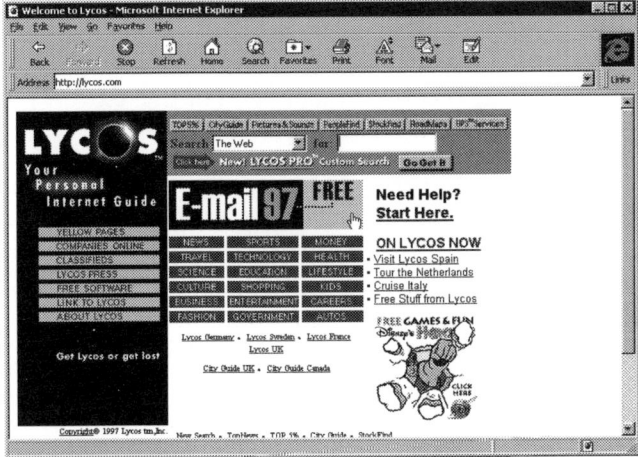

The popular Lycos page includes 18 subheadings to help you find just about anything quickly

The Best of the Rest

Amazing Environmental Organization Webdirectory
http://www.webdirectory.com/
An eco-friendly site that gives eco-friendly links.

Argus/University of Michigan Clearinghouse
http://www.lib.umich.edu/
This engine has an academic bias, good place to look up things with long unpronounceable names.

Shareware.com
http://www.shareware.com/
One of the top sites for finding and downloading free or inexpensive software. Either browse around, or use a key word search to find the type of program you need easily.

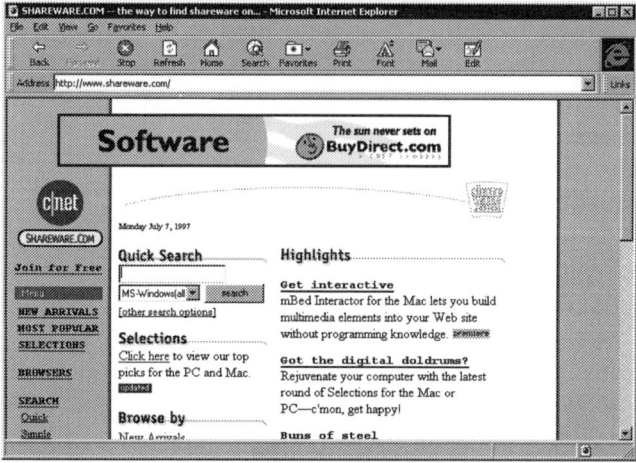

A slice of software heaven at Shareware.com

Deja News
http://www.dejanews.com/
An engine devoted to searching Usenet. Whether you're looking for a newsgroup covering a particular subject, or messages that include your key words, Deja News will help you find what you need.

Excite
http://www.excite.com/
Excite has the usual search facilities but also allows you to search by 'concept'. This is much the same as key word, but it's worth a try.

Gamelan
http://www.gamelan.com/
One of the hottest sites around for fans of Java, a new language used to create interactive games, animations and controls that add spice to web pages.

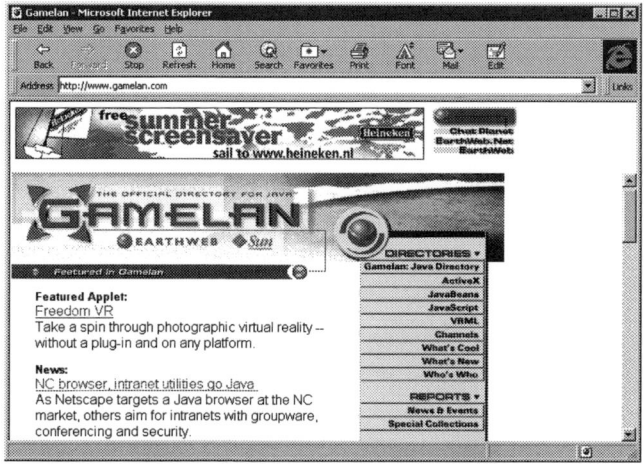

Experience the very latest in Web technology at Gamelan

GNN Select
http://gnn.com/
GNN reviews the best sites on the Net. If you agree with the review this place will be heaven.

G.O.D.
http://www.gold.net/
No, not *that* God, but the Global Online Directory, allows you to add your own site instantly.

CHAPTER 9 ▽ Search engines

Hotbot
http://www.hotbot.com/

IBM Informarket
http://www.infomkt.ibm.com/
Commercial information.

Infoseek Guide
http://guide.infoseek.com/
Traditional search engine with extra bits, such as the ability to search the Internet for people's names.

Nerdworld Media Internet Subject Index
http://www.nerdworld.com/
Allows you to set up your own search indexes for newsgroups and Web sites.

100 Hot Websites
http://www.web21.com/
The top 10 (plus 90) Web sites every week – a good way to find out what everyone else is looking at (and avoiding it because it will be very slow).

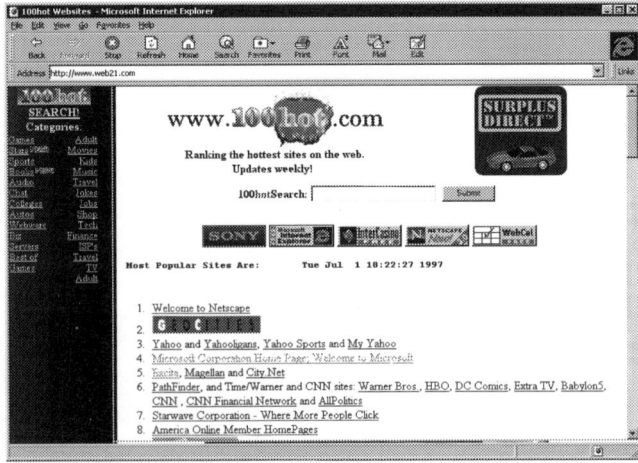

The 100 hottest sites on the web, plus a useful categorised search engine

▽ The Best of the Rest

Open Text Index
http://www.opentext.com/
This engine claims to search every word on the Internet.
Madness.

Point
http://www.pointcom.com/
Another reviews based site – gives its top 10 (best) sites every week.

Starting Point
http://www.stpt.com/
A search engine that has more news and business-based categories.

Webcrawler
http://webcrawler.com/
Relatively normal search engine, but likes to show up new and unusual sites as well.

W3 Servers
http://www.w3.org/
This is the home page of the World Wide Web Consortium and is a good place to go to find about the Web.

What's New
http://www.orst.edu/aw/stygui/whatsnew.html
What's new (on the Internet).

Whowhere?
http://whowhere.com/
Resource to help you find people or organizations on the web.

CHAPTER 10

Suggested Web sites

There are thousands of places to visit on the Web – if you're looking for something special, then you're best to search using one of our recommended search engines – so back to the previous chapter with you. But here's a taste of what you can find out there, divided by sections. We've tried to pick useful sites. And if they aren't finished yet (as much of the internet isn't), at least they're interesting.

▽ Suggested Web sites 81

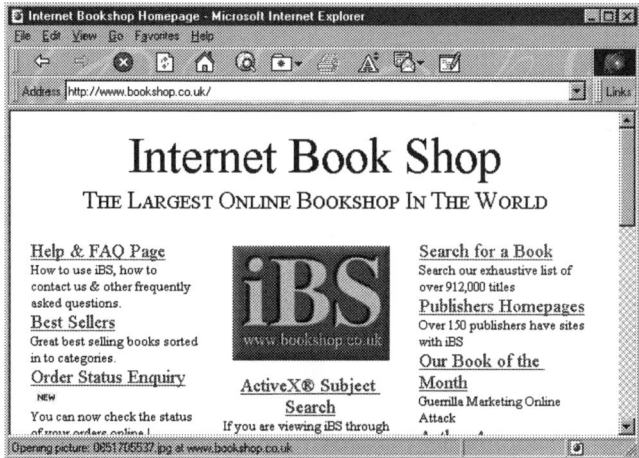

Browse or search for a book, and order it online

No FT.com, no comment

CHAPTER 10 ▽ Suggested Web sites

Buy and sell for free at Loot's advanced but easy-to-use site

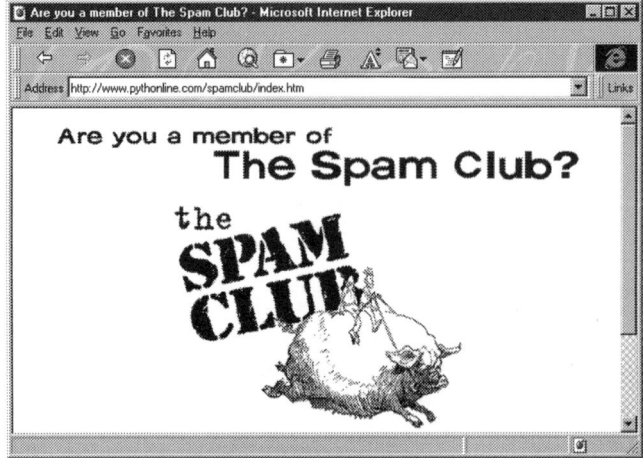

Where Monty Python fans can find anything they want . . .

▽ Suggested Web sites 83

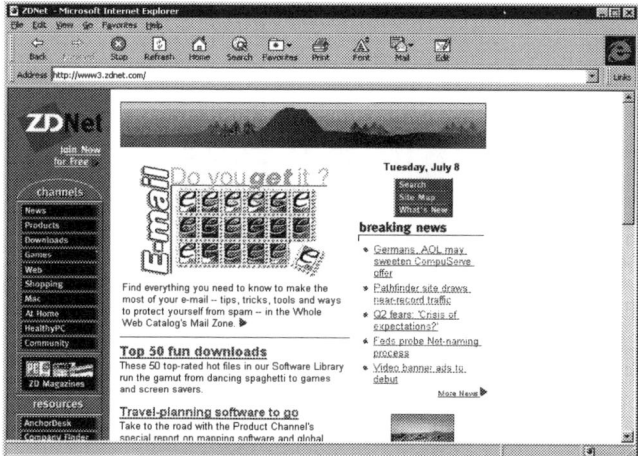

Ziff Davis' useful site for computer software and news, along with excellent Driver Finder and Tip Finder sections

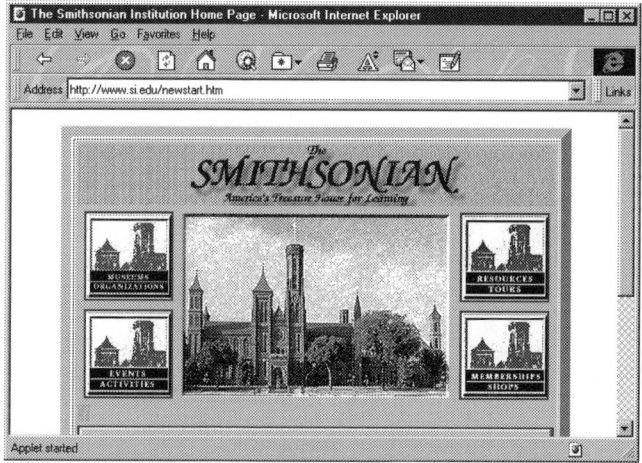

Take a tour of The Smithsonian Institute, America's 'treasure house' online

84 CHAPTER 10 ▽ **Suggested Web sites**

Get immediate answers to all those nagging scientific questions

Help, advice and resources for graduates planning their next move

▽ **Suggested Web sites**

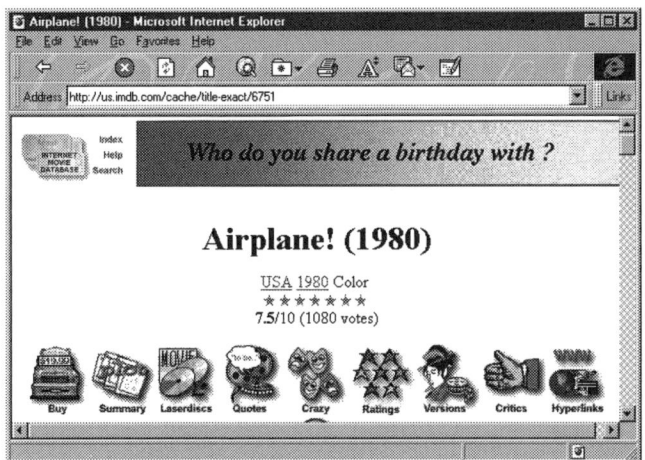

The UK's own Internet Movie Database is packed with news, reviews and movie trivia

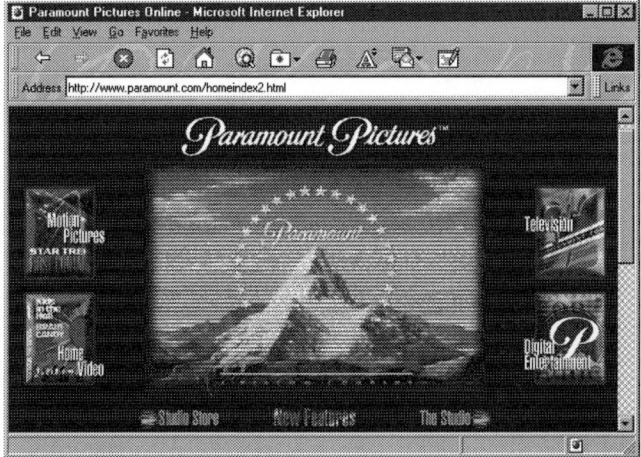

Paramount want you to watch their Pictures. After seeing this site, you won't be able to resist!

CHAPTER 10 ▽ Suggested Web sites

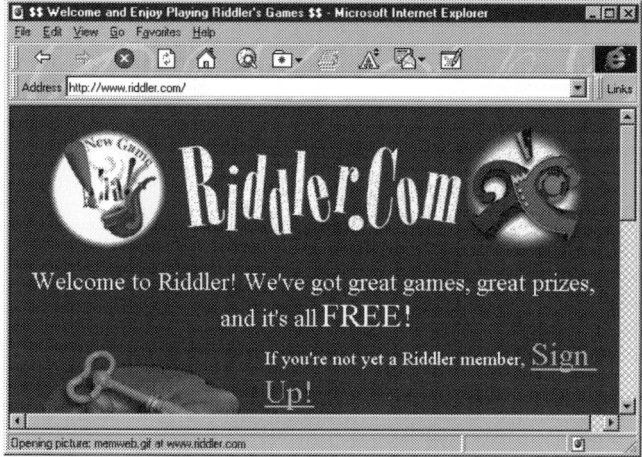

Play brain-teasing games online at Ridler.com

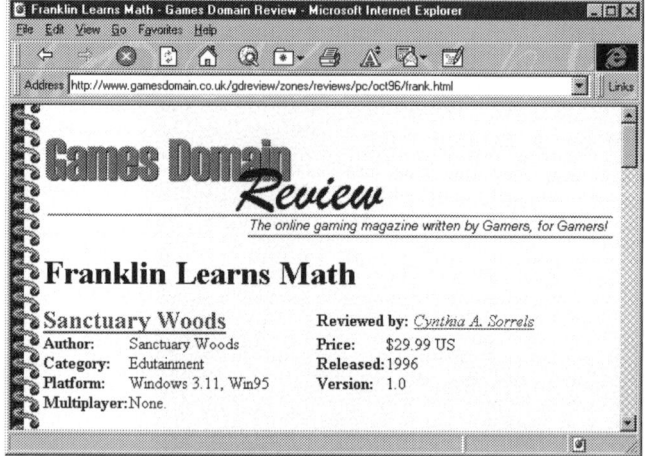

Keep up with the latest computer games at Games Domain

▽ **Suggested Web sites**

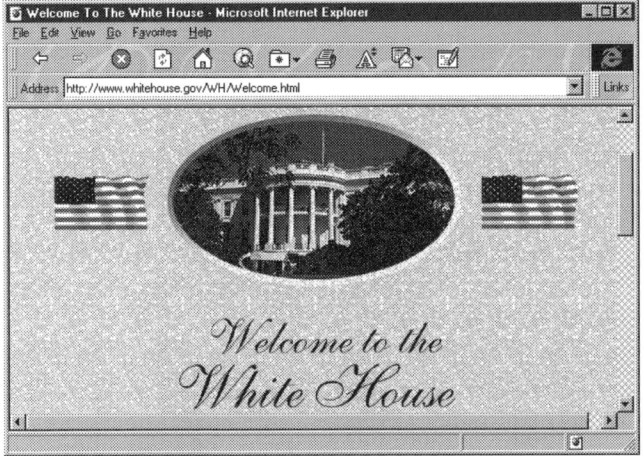

Take a tour of the White House, e-mail the President, and meet Socks the cat

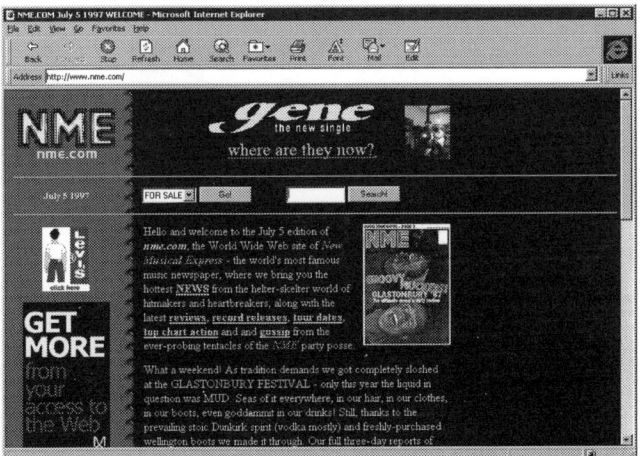

The latest news from the rock world at New Musical Express

CHAPTER 10 ▽ Suggested Web sites

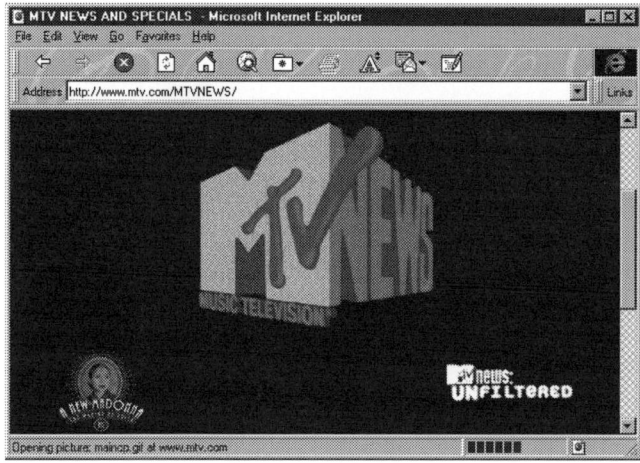

MTV: a cool place for the hip to hop

The top UK financial site for professionals and beginners alike

▽ Suggested Web sites

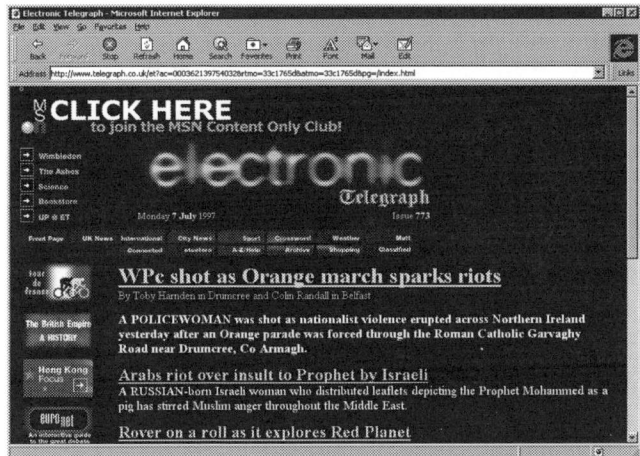
Read the Daily Telegraph's stylish online incarnation

Track down your dream date at Deadline

CHAPTER 10 ▽ Suggested Web sites

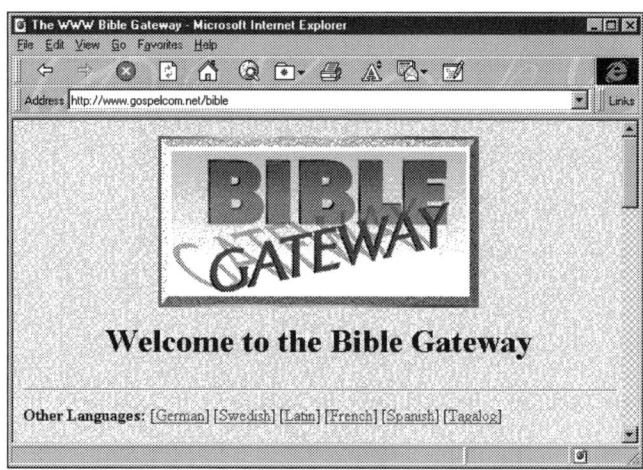

The ultimate multi-language, multi-version Bible lookup

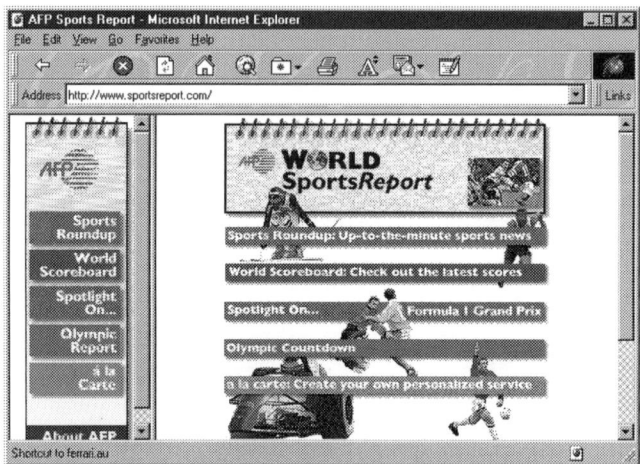

News and features covering every sport imaginable

▽ **Books**

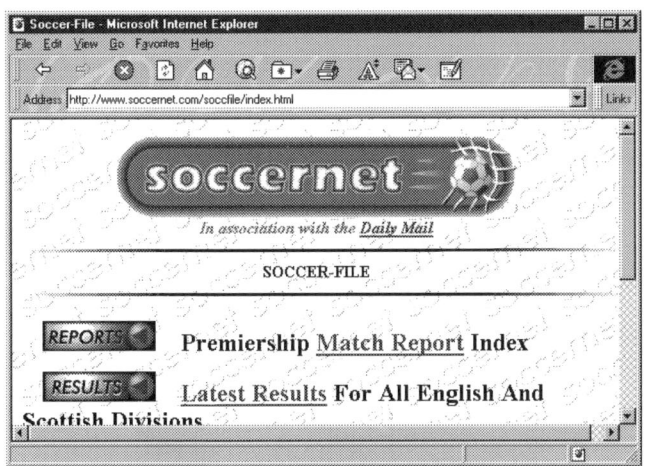

Regularly updated with the latest football results, news and views

Books

Internet Bookshop
http://www.bookshop.co.uk/
A million books, so you can't possibly have read all of them. This UK site has the opportunity to search by author or key word, check out the best sellers, read about the book of the month and, of course, buy the stock.

Internet Public Library
http://ipl.sils.umich.edu/
One of those ambitious projects you find on the Web, the Internet public library sets out to be a reference – for everything. Arranged in sections like health and commerce, it'll answer a lot of questions, but it's no surprise to find that it isn't finished yet ...

Books On-Line
http://www.cs.cmu.edu/Web/books.html

CHAPTER 10 ▽ Suggested Web sites

If you want to give up paper completely, you need to know where to find books that have been posted on the Web. This will tell you – and there are a surprising number of them. All types of books, from children's books to anarchist literature, plus foreign language stuff too.

HarperCollins Interactive
http://www.harpercollins.com/hci/index.htm
News about the latest books, information about books being published on CD-ROM, even a user survey – the interactive division of HarperCollins has everything that the bibliophile needs, plus some great design.

Internet Talking Bookshop
http://www.orma.co.uk/intabs.htm
The bookshop for you, if you're looking for the classics on tape. If you don't like classics, there's *Star Trek* and Danielle Steele too.

Prentice Hall
http://www.prenhall.com/
The publishers of this book, and one of the world's largest educational publishers, and their site – well designed with heavy use of graphics, animation and frames – is based on the catalogue. It goes much further than that though, with Web sites offering further information for some of the books, a guide to Prentice Hall authors, and even a section telling you how to become an author yourself. The authors of this book like this site very much.

Amazon.com
http://www.amazon.com
Proclaims itself to be "the Earth's biggest bookstore", and it's probably not wrong.

Spawn
http://www.mcfarlane.com
What? Actually, it's the best-selling comic book.

Travel Books
http://www.travelbooks.co.uk
Opinionated site – only the books the Webmaster likes are listed!

Philip K. Dick
http://host.interloc.com/~iliadbks/pkd.html
The author who gave us *Blade Runner* and *Total Recall.*

Pulp Faction
http://www.pulpfact.demon.co.uk/
Check out what's next in literary fashion.

Business and Money

Loot
http://www.loot.com
If you live in the south of England you will know Loot as a fat newspaper packed with classified advertisements selling everything from houses to hatstands. This is a fat Web site packed with advertisements from the paper selling everything...you know the drill. Browse the ads, place your own (it's free), search for that particular item you suddenly cannot live without.

Shoppers Universe
http://www.shoppersuniverse.com/
Great Universal's presence on the Web is distinguished by a regular online auction, featuring computer software and hardware and even items from the catalogue, like mountain bikes. The online shop has 4000 items, covering technology, clothes, toys and sports.

Investor's Edge
http://www.investorsedge.com/
A huge site and an essential if you want to follow your shares. Reports, prices, the chance to create a portfolio and see how it performs, plus a real-time stock ticker and analyst reports. It's optimized for Microsoft browsers; there's extra

CHAPTER 10 ▽ Suggested Web sites

content if anyone using a Microsoft-based browser subscribes.

Reuter's Business Headlines
http://www.yahoo.com/headlines/business/
Provided as an enhancement to Yahoo, the directory listing of top Internet sites, the business headlines give you all the news in digestible, bite-size packages. The news is prompt and changes regularly, but it does have a US slant.

FT.com
http://www.ft.com/
The Financial Times hits the Web with a high-quality Web site. The site contains news from the newspaper, has quick response times and a European slant that makes an antidote to the US-based Web content of most sites. The usual high standard of the FT reporting is yours for free – after you fill in the exhaustive registration questionnaire.

Wall Street Journal
http://wsj.com/
'The most trusted business newspaper in the world' comes to the Internet in a subscription service, with a scrolling stock ticker, all the content from the printed version and some advanced design. The old-fashioned look of the paper-based version doesn't translate to the Web, and the interactive version certainly isn't pretty, but it's deep.

UK Business Index
http://www.ukbusinessindex.com/
Business news and advice for Brits in an accessible format. There are 15 sections covering most vertical markets, and if you register (it's free) they will send you a free e-mail newsletter. Great value, quality local content.

PeopleBank
http://www.peoplebank.com
Employment agency – it's British.

Résumé writing
http://www.wm.edu/csrv/career/stualum/resmdir/contents.html
How to compile a good CV.

MoneyWorld UK
http://www.moneyworld.co.uk
A brilliant UK personal finance web site.

Comedy

Joke of the day
http://allworld.net/allworld/jokes/awjokes.html
Some are good, some are particularly lame, but the great thing about this service is that you know there will always be another one along tomorrow – except, as it says, at weekends.

ComedyWeb
http://www.comedyweb.co.uk/
The source of choice if you want to know about UK standup comedy. A handsome site with profiles, interviews, reviews and competitions, this has all the depth of a good magazine.

Pythonline
http://www.pythonline.com/
Not surprisingly the internet is full of people who know the 'Dead Parrot' sketch backwards and will quote it at you given half the chance. If you are one of these people, find kindred spirits at this mass of Pythonesque pages, including the Spam Club, Gumby barmaid, silly commands, and pointless links.

CHAPTER 10 ▽ Suggested Web sites

Wall-o-shame
http://www.milk.com/wall-o-shame/
Appalling true stories, advertisements and articles collected as a sign that the world is truly going mad and the apocalypse is truly upon us. The laughs die in your throat as you read about the white supremacist who wanted to be called 'Hi Hitler' at his trial (he thought that's what people said to Hitler when they saluted), and the Canadian government policy document on the legality of boot licking.

Migraine Boy
http://www.migraineboy.com/
Another off-beat comic strip. Very odd.

Carry On
http://www.adavids.demon.co.uk/carry/carry.html
Infamy, infamy they've all got it...you know the rest.

Light Bulb Jokes
http://www.cyberhighway.net/~kn1ght/jokes/light.bulbs.html
http://www.cwrl.utexas.edu/~claire/texts/lightbulb.html
How many software technical support people does it take to change a lightbulb? I think you'll find that's a hardware problem sir.

The Secret Diary of Bill Gates
http://www.tiac.net/users/billg40/main/

Ask Mr. Angst –
http://www.utm.edu/~jfieser/angst.htm

Dear Xavier Landers –
http://www1.mhv.net/~guito/advicef.htm

Computing

UK Internet Directory
http://www.ukdirectory.com/
The trouble with most directory listings isn't that they find too little, they find too much. If you are tired of finding the Web site you want, only to find it's carefully tailored for the Polish market, you'll relish this directory of links for sites based in the UK. All the categories are here, and response times are swift.

Shareware.com
http://www.shareware.com/
Where do you find the shareware (that's downloadable software to you and me) you need? This site has a reference for every bit of software on the Web, with a description of the packages, charts of the most popular downloads, and the download sites listed by country, and more importantly, rated for reliability.

ZDNet
http://www.zdnet.com
Ziff Davis is the world's largest publisher of computer news, notably for the techie's standard-bearer *PC Magazine*. It's no surprise to find that ZDNet has a huge range of services, allowing you to search for articles by key word, look at a range of jobs offered, find out about the latest trade shows – even use a customizable technology news service to make your own 'Daily Me'.

Versions
http://www.versions.com/
If you want to keep in touch with the latest releases of your software, there's two ways to do it: either you scour the computer press, talk to your friends, phone your software supplier once a week and peer in shop windows; or you go to this Web site, tell it which software you use, and it will send you a mail message when you need to upgrade. The Web in 'life made easier' shock.

CHAPTER 10 ▽ Suggested Web sites

Microsoft
http://www.microsoft.com/uk
Not surprisingly Microsoft's Web site is vast: news, white papers, 'how to' guides, technical support and free software to download. It's fast, up to date, and it looks great – especially as it is optimized for your browser. If you get bored listening to hold music while waiting for technical support, all the support files that Microsoft's staff use can be searched on line too.

Check out some other self-explanatory and useful home pages at:
http://www.lotus.com
http://www.intel.com
http://www.ibm.com
http://www.compaq.com
http://www.wordperfect.com
http://www.apple.com
If you are looking for a computer company on line, try the simple formula: www+name+com – your chance of success is roughly 80 per cent!

Culture

National Museum of Film, Photography and Television
http://www.nmsi.ac.uk/nmpft/
Bradford's fine museum doesn't get the coverage it deserves, perhaps because it is oop North and so it's off the tourist track. On the Internet, this collection of information, details of projects and the screening times for the museum's giant IMAX cinema are only a minute away.

Smithsonian Institution
http://www.si.edu/
America's largest cultural institution is 150 years old, and it's still as strong as ever. Not just a museum, the Smithsonian covers a number of collections, libraries and conservation projects. See the site for the evidence that the Smithsonian really is 'America's Treasure House'.

The Louvre
http://mistral.culture.fr/louvre/louvrea.htm
You don't have to go to Paris to see the collection of its greatest Art Gallery. Not everything that you would see in the real gallery is here, but The Louvre site has images of many of its most famous paintings, as well as a history of the Louvre itself, and background detail about the collections. A multilingual site, unfortunately not all of it is translated into English.

Literary Calendar
http://www.yasuda-u.ac.jp/LitCalendar.html
On this day . . . find out what happened on this elegant Japanese site (don't worry, it's in English). A simple idea, but interesting and surprising. There's space for you to add suggestions too.

Shakespeare and the Globe
http://shakespeare.eb.com/shakespeare/index2.html
This is an encyclopaedic site, perhaps not surprisingly since it's a part of the Encyclopaedia Britannica online at www.eb.com. Fans and students will find plenty of information here about the Bard, his plays, and the Globe Theatre.

UK Club Map
http://137.222.84.160/uk-clubs/clubmap.htm
A different sort of culture – reviews, locations, DJs for the UK nightclub scene.

Education

New Scientist
http://www.newscientist.com/
An award-winner from the UK's leading science magazine, *Planet Science* has a lighter edge than the printed version, while retaining its authority. If you want to find out the

answer to questions like 'Why do biscuits go soft when they are left out, but bread goes hard?', here's the place.

Discovery Channel Online
http://www.discovery.com/
If you have satellite TV you'll know the Discovery Channel: here's a Web site that not only tells you what's on, but gives you background information too. Presented with a tabloid relish that suits Web browsing, you'll find anything from the *Titanic* to robots thrown together in a boffin's lucky dip.

Internet for Learning
http://www.rmplc.co.uk/
A UK-based site hosted by educational computer specialist Research Machines, this has a more academic feel to it. It's less jazzy and less fun, but there's depth, and support for the national curriculum in the subjects covered.

Educate Online
http://www.educate.co.uk/
Terrible design, great content. A grab bag of links, reviews, lists and competitions covering everything in education. Especially good for parents.

Interactive Frog Dissection
http://curry.edschool.virginia.edu/~insttech/frog
It's not a misprint. A cult favourite, even if you don't have a dead frog handy to follow the step-by-step instructions. If you do, it is even better.

NUS Online
http://www.nus.org.uk/
If the Net is full of students, here's a place for them to go. Serious-minded.

Arachnomania
http://www.mcs.com/~spider/arachnomania.html
If you like spiders, you'll love this.

Employment

Online Career Centre
http://www.occ.com/
A massive repository of jobs world wide, with links to agencies too. The database is searchable, and despite being US-based, throws up a number of UK-based jobs, as well as opportunities in Europe.

CareerWeb
http://www.cweb.com/
Books, tools and advice if you are changing job; even better if you are changing your career. More US-oriented, so you may find it a little rich for your blood when discussing management theory, but a valuable jumping-off point.

CareerNet UK
http://www.ipl.co.uk/recruit.html
A Brit-based careers advice page, more down-to-earth and practical than its US counterparts, and with plenty of resources and opportunities for UK-based jobseekers. There are questionnaires, worksheets and advice sections for employers. A fine start if you don't have a job. Even better if you don't know which job you want.

Gradunet
http://www.gradunet.co.uk/
Another UK site, this time to offer graduate opportunities. There's even a Hall of Fame for grads who got jobs or training places using the site, and it's a well-designed set of pages offering advice and contacts as well as jobs.

Jobs in the UK
http://www.pikeperry.co.uk/ppp/career/
A no-frills site, without the pretty graphics, but with a huge list of agencies that use the Web for recruiting, as well as sites to which you can e-mail your CV. Short on advice, but long on places to go and get advice. Or indeed, a job.

CHAPTER 10 ▽ Suggested Web sites

Games

The Games Domain
http://www.gamesdomain.co.uk/
Reviews, downloads, hints, demos, and recently redesigned to be on the cutting edge of the Web, this UK-hosted site has the added benefit that it is optimized for Microsoft's browser. Your first stop if games are your bag.

Entertainment Online
http://www.e-on.com/
Sophisticated site, self-proclaimed as 'Absolutely the best games site in the world'. Top quality graphics, games from Sega and Sony, and even a 'virtual casino'.

Id Software
http://www.idsoftware.com/
If you've played any PC games over the last two years, you'll know about Id software. First Doom brought offices to a standstill, then Quake moved the battle to the Internet. All the information, the downloads and the release dates for the games that give Net users the chance to kill each other in bloodthirsty virtual reality.

Riddler
http://www.riddler.com/
Exceptional 'mind games' site, with great design and animations backing up a series of free puzzles. There's trivia, crosswords, a cryptic whodunnit, even the chance to match your wits against fellow visitors in 'King of the Hill'. Be warned – it's addictive.

Gamespot
http://www.gamespot.com/
Games magazine with lots of graphics and a busy design (there's a graphics-free version if the site gets too slow). All the news, reviews and demos of the latest games. New games get a walk-through, and if you get stuck, this site has hints and cheats too.

Government

All three major parties now have remarkably similar web sites (what does this tell us?), but all give you the chance to contact government and practice democracy Internet style:

The Labour Party
http://www.labour.org.uk/

The Conservative Party
http://www.conservative-party.org.uk/

The Liberal Democratic Party
http://www.libdems.org.uk/

CCTA Government Information
http://www.open.gov.uk/
Large and comprehensive set of pages on government authorities, this marks a new high point in worthiness. Unlikely to win any awards for design, but for research and access to basic information, telephone numbers and press releases, it's hard to fault.

The White House
http://www.whitehouse.gov
The US government invented the information superhighway, so it's no surprise to find them getting on to it. Take a good look round the famous building, read about what's happening in US government.

No. 10 Downing Street
http://www.number-10.gov.uk/
Take a guided tour around this famous address, read biographies of past Prime Ministers, sign the visitors' book, and see a picture of a rather surprised cat named Humphrey.

CHAPTER 10 ▽ Suggested Web sites

Music

NME.com
http://www.nme.com/
If you haven't read NME for a while, you won't be surprised to find that it's still the same, on or off the Web: lots of bands, reviews, record shop advertisements and T-shirts. But here you can download snippets of this week's singles, chat with other music fans on line, and not worry that the ink will come off on your hands.

MTV Online
http://www.mtv.com/
As befits the giant of American rock music, this has a front page with a huge graphic on it that takes 10 minutes to download. Once you're past that there's a well-designed Web site which will inform you rather than inspire you, with some fun animations and samples.

Atlantic Records
http://www.atlantic-records.com/
All the big record companies have their own sites, and this one is a good example, with more than you could ever want to know about bands starting with All-4-One and ending with Zoo People. You'll meet anyone from the Pet Shop Boys to Spew on the way. Check out the Freebies section for some excellent competition prizes.

Pathfinder
http://pathfinder.com/
Is this a music site, a news site or an entertainment site? It's all of them, and more. Time Warner on line collects music reviews and features in a densely packed magazine format.

Classic CD
http://www.futurenet.co.uk/
Find this UK-based classical music magazine on FutureNet, the Web site of its publisher. As well as reviews and listings,

there's a lot of information on building a hi-fi system, famous classical composers and access to other classical music sites.

Pastel Blue
http://www.demon.co.uk/pastel/ukdir
UK CD supplier with huge specialist sections among its 100 000 compact disks. Search the catalogue by artist, title or label to find those special titles that you just can't get hold of in your local shop.

CD World
http://www.cdworld.com/
Extremely slick US CD supplier that offers games, cassettes and videos in its 170 000 stock items. US prices mean you can pick up a bargain. The catalogue lists release dates, makes recommendations and flags limited editions and rarities.

Spin Magazine
http://www.musicblvd.com
Top music mag from the US.

Virgin Radio
http://www.virginradio.co.uk
Top quality site, with audio.

Internet Beatles album and Beatles info
http://www.liv.ac.uk/ipm/beatles/
http://entertainmentweb.com/

Newspapers

MSNBC
http://www.msnbc.com/
As the title suggests, the 24-hour rolling news page that's a combination of the best efforts of US network NBC and Microsoft. This points to the custom news page, where you are served the news that you want – you specify it once by

CHAPTER 10 ▽ Suggested Web sites

filling in a form, and every time you visit the page afterwards, it is already set up for you.

Electronic Telegraph
http://www.telegraph.co.uk/
The first British newspaper to go on the web, the ET has continued to upgrade its coverage to keep ahead of the pack. Now there are classifieds, a bookshop, good links to related sites and, of course, Fantasy football league.

PA News
http://www.pa.press.net/
Read the news before it hits the newspapers – PA is a news agency, which means that many of the stories you read in tomorrow's press are found by PA today. A well-designed site, fast and easy to navigate, and unusually for the Web, a UK bias.

CNN Interactive
http://www.cnn.com/
The best 24-hour rolling news site, CNN has an excellent technology page, superb in-depth coverage and lots of links to other sites. When there's a big news story breaking, CNN's Web coverage can leave TV news standing.

The Times
http://www.the-times.co.uk/
One site, two newspapers – *The Times* and *The Sunday Times* share a site, including all the news, good features, and even the crossword. The layout mimics the printed page, so if you are not used to reading news on-screen, start here.

Electronic Newsstand
http://www.enews.com/
More than 2000 newspaper and magazine links.

Guardian OnLine
http://go2.guardian.co.uk
Dedicated to republishing only the OnLine (technology) section of *The Guardian*, but with a good archive.

Personals

Dateline UK
http://www.dateline.uk.com/
A fun site, with the chance to do a search in the database for someone you might like to meet by specifying a place on the map and a few preferences. But you won't be able to make any contacts unless you join – which of course, you can do using the site.

Cupid's Network
http://www.cupidnet.com/
The mother of all personal dating services, US-based Cupid not only carries its own woman and man of the month (!) but also has a number of links to rated affiliate sites, plus an online bookstore – offering a free copy of *How to build a Lasting Relationship* to download.

Match.com
http://www.match.com
Claims the crown as the biggest single online dating agency with 100 000 members, and it's certainly a good-looking site, offering a free 10-day trial and membership for only $7.95 a month afterwards. You're selecting from a US-biased database, but there are UK entries too.

Radio, Film and TV

Cyberville Radio
http://www.cyberville.co.uk
A Web-based radio station – it sounds mad, but it isn't. Visit the site, pick a programme (there are eight half-hour slots updated daily), and browse away, with Cyberville downloading and playing in the background. The programmes are a lightweight mix of music and chat, and are actually rather good.

Interactive TV Guide
http://www.yearling.com/

CHAPTER 10 ▽ Suggested Web sites

It's hell looking through all the pages of programmes for the week, then finding the programme you wanted to see – half an hour after it's finished. This site provides an end to multi-channel programme missing misery by allowing you to select only the programmes and channels you are interested in – then serving up a daily list of what you might want to watch. Last week's lottery numbers are there too.

Paramount Pictures
http://www.paramount.com/
A site combining news and previews of Paramount's films, TV programmes and videos. Some of the dedicated sites for Hollywood's blockbuster movies are breathtaking – as long as you have a fast enough web connection. And of course there's the official site for . . .

Star Trek
http://www.dimensionx.com/people/jsbell/Star_Trek/
Where would the Internet be without Trekkers? There are hundreds of sites (including an online Klingon language institute), but this site, designed and built by a dedicated fan, combines the best links with some surprisingly informed content. It almost makes Trekkerdom respectable.

Internet Movie database
http://uk.imdb.com/
The Web's most informative database and a shining example of how wonderful an internet collaboration can be, this massive database of movie trivia, ratings, information and reviews began its life at Cardiff University. Now also hosted in the US, every piece of cinema information you need is here, from the name of the Best Boy upwards.

Mr Showbiz
http://www.mrshowbiz.com
Hollywood gossip, rumours and reviews. Scurrilous, trivial and very well informed, Mr Showbiz gives you the inside information on the stars.

Channel 4
http://www.channel4.co.uk
Listings, features, Zig and Zag.

Cinemania OnLine
http://www.msn.com/cinemania/
Not as all-encompassing as the Internet Movie Database, but good content.

Religion

A Christian Introduction to the Web
http://www.geocities.com/Athens/6882/christinfo.html
Actually it's mostly an introduction to the Web, and not a bad one, with a bunch of Christian links at the bottom of the page. The links are well-researched, and if you're not religious, the general information might be useful too.

WWW Bible Gateway
http://www.gospelcom.net/bible
Search the Bible – or seven different versions of the Bible to be more accurate – in six languages for words and phrases. The concordances give extremely fast results.

Man is Man Made
http://www.flex.net/~terran/
The UK's resource for atheists, this fair-minded site lacks content of its own but makes up for it with a host of links to the flourishing US-based Internet atheist community. There are also links to relevant Usenet discussion groups.

Comparative Religion
http://weber.u.washington.edu/~madin/
An interesting collection of links if you have a year of your life spare to follow them all, covering all aspects of religion: faiths are divided into Eastern and Western, and there are special sections on women, tolerance, scripture, art, music and other aspects of religious life.

CHAPTER 10 ▽ Suggested Web sites

Vatican Radio
http://www.wrn.org
If you want to hear the Church of Rome party line, you can find its shortwave frequency on this page – or download a 15 minute daily news broadcast, or a 20 minute feature to play back on your PC. Vatican Radio has been broadcasting since 1931 (not always on the Web though). If you're a Catholic, you'll want to take heed of its injunction to 'Listen for Heaven's Sake'.

Spirit-WWW
http://www.spiritweb.org/
Half Buddhism, half X-Files, this new age site is a fascinating mix of the profound and the barmy, and it is not always easy to tell which is which. Specialist subjects range from reincarnation and faith healing to UFOs.

Sport

World Sports Report
http://www.sportsreport.com/
Hosted by Agence-France Presse, this eclectic mix of every sport imaginable still manages to catch the important headlines of the day, while providing special features, a diary and spotlights. The quality of writing and presentation is high.

FIFA Online
http://www.fifa.com/index.html
World football for addicts, with all you need to know about FIFA's members, world rankings, press releases, and a survey to find out your opinions about football. You can't guarantee they'll do anything about it, but at least you can let off steam.

ESPN SportZone
http://espnet.sportszone.com/
Glitzy site which mirrors the fast-forward style of ESPN,

America's cable sports channel. If you like American sport, you'll love this site, with its relish for detail and snappy, well-informed writing. If you don't like the word soccer and think that baseball is rounders for men, give this one a miss.

Soccernet

http://www.soccernet.com/

Despite the title, a UK site with everything the Premier League fan needs for relaxation. Features, match reports, links to other sites, and the opportunity to subscribe to an e-mail list.

Sydney 2000

http://www.sydney.olympic.org/

Preparations for the millennial Olympiad are underway already, and the Web site was one of the first things to go up! Read about what's happening in this bright, quick site. Bookmark it, watch it grow and slow down as everyone else finds it too.

Sports Chat!

http://www.4-lane.com/sportschat/

As a sports fan, you like to talk about your interest. What do you do if you're the only one in your house who likes backpacking or ice hockey? You log in to this service with its unorthodox collection of unusual sports to talk about. Register and they will send you an email when a scheduled chat is being planned.

CHAPTER 11

You want software? We got software – downloading

What do you do if you want to buy some software? At the moment, you probably go to a shop and ask the person behind the counter for it. Provided it is in stock, and you don't have to get back in the car and drive to the next shop, you hand over some money, and get a box the size of a breeze block in return. You go home, undo the shrink wrap, pull out the manuals, the registration forms, the unexplained bit of cardboard that everyone seems to put in the box for fun, and find the diskettes or the CD-ROM. You open the installation manual, follow the instructions, install the software and, provided nothing goes wrong, it's installed on your computer. There must be a better way.

There is.

Software isn't the box, the manuals, or the bit of cardboard. It isn't even the diskettes. It's the information on those diskettes, and that can be copied from one computer to another using the telephone wires. Of course, we know how to do that, because that's what happens on the Internet.

Unfortunately it will be a long time before your word processor or your spreadsheet is bought on the Internet. Software like Microsoft Office is so huge that you would be copying it for the best part of a day over the average Internet connection. What you can get, though, are smaller utilities, gadgets to make your computer work better, games, fixes for problems with your existing software, and some software upgrades. Much of this stuff is free; most of it is free to try out. The Internet is a bran tub. There's a lot of bran in it, but reach in far enough, and there are prizes too.

Some History: Why you Can Get Software for Free

When the personal computer was invented, there wasn't any software for it, but there were a lot of hippies who could write software. Some of them turned into businessmen and sold their software in colourful boxes in high street shops. Others decided that the best way for as many people as possible to see their software was to let anyone copy it and use it, but ask them to pay for it if they carried on using it. Sure, some people wouldn't pay up, but you would still do better than having to pay for wholesalers and adverts in magazines. This is the concept of shareware.

Shareware's a natural for the Internet, where it can be copied all over the globe and interested would-be users can download it. Today, a lot of shareware is protected, so it stops working after 30 days, or doesn't save more than a certain number of files. But there's more of it around than ever. Without the idea of shareware, we'd never have had the World Wide Web, because the Web browser you're using now is distributed as shareware.

CHAPTER 11 ▽ You want software?

Let's Go and Find Some Software Then

You obtain software using File Transfer Protocol, or FTP. We don't need to care what this means: just recognize that when we're talking FTP, we mean a file travelling from one computer to another over the Net. Files are stored in 'archives' – hard disks that contain compressed versions of all the software to download. Often these archives are provided out of goodwill by universities or companies with some excess disk capacity; remember when looking for software that you are using a free resource, and exercise responsibility.

There are two ways to get software by FTP: an easy way and a hard way.

The Easy Way

Fire up your Web browser and head off for http://www.shareware.com.

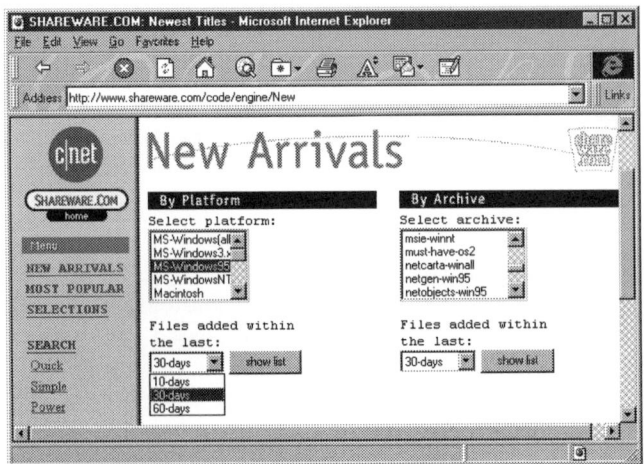

Shareware.com – the indispensable software source

▽ Let's Go and Find Some Software Then

This is a remarkable resource detailing a number of software sites from which you can download. Find a program you want by searching the listing at the site, and follow the links to download: shareware.com will deposit you at an FTP site, where you will see the software you can download displayed as a text list. Click on the name of the program you want, and the browser will put up a box asking you where you want to save it on your hard disk.

Type in the directory and filename you want the program to be stored as, and it will download to your hard disk. This can take 30 minutes for a really large program, like a Web browser or a game, so don't panic. You can also go off and surf other sites while the file is downloading, but don't stop the download until it is complete, because you cannot pick up where you left off.

The Hard(er) Way

You can't find everything using the Web. Sometimes you may want to use a technique called 'anonymous FTP'. Your ISP will usually provide a program (which itself is likely to be shareware, believe it or not) to enable you to connect direct to

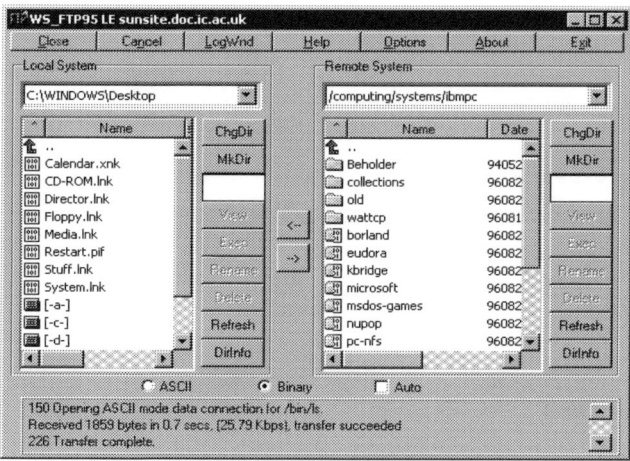

WS_FTP, an extremely popular FTP program from http://www.ipswitch.com/

an FTP site. This is a much quicker route if you are forever having to download software from the same place.

If your using WS_FTP (pictured), you set up an FTP session by typing the URL of the site you want to visit into the Session Profile box that appears when you start the program. Many are similar to the Web address of the site. For example, www.microsoft.com has an FTP archive called ftp.microsoft.com; but this is not a hard and fast rule. If in doubt, explore using the Web browser first. You will find a number of FTP sites listed on the Net. We've given you a few to start off with at the end of the chapter.

There are other boxes, but what matter are the two called 'User ID' and 'Password'. Anonymous FTP is 'public access' FTP – anyone can log in; your User ID is 'anonymous'. Your password is, confusingly, your e-mail address.

Connect to the Internet, and run the session you have just saved. You are then connected directly to the remote computer via the Internet. You will see two directory and file listings. On the left should be your hard disk. On the right, the hard disk of the FTP site. Highlight the file you want to copy from the remote system, and select the directory you wish to copy it to on your hard disk. Hit the button marked with a left-pointing arrow.

The file should copy as before. The same process is used in reverse when you copy files to your Web space to set up your own Web page (see Chapter 13), although that's not anonymous FTP: your service provider will give you a password, so that only you can access that site.

Where's the Catch?

Of course there has to be a catch. There are several.

1. *You don't know what you are getting.* Just because a program looks like it is what you want, doesn't mean that

▽ Where's the Catch?

is the case. For example, if something is described as 'the best word processor ever', that might be wrong. In fact, it almost certainly will be. It might not even be a word processor. Commercial sites are usually accurate in their descriptions, but the same cannot be said of privately held archives.

2. *Watch out for viruses.* Getting duff software is a disappointment you can live with. Getting a virus over the internet is potentially far more dangerous.

It's important to realize that you have no more reassurance that what you are downloading is legitimate than the word of someone on the Internet who you have never met. Software contains executable files: executable files can carry viruses. Ordinary Web browsing does not transfer this type of executable file, which is why the Internet hasn't destroyed every computer in the country.

There's only two sure ways to guard against viruses: download nothing, or buy an anti-virus product that watches for downloaded viruses.

Some popular anti-virus sites are:

Dr Solomon's – `http://www.drsolomon.com`
The original and still one of the best.

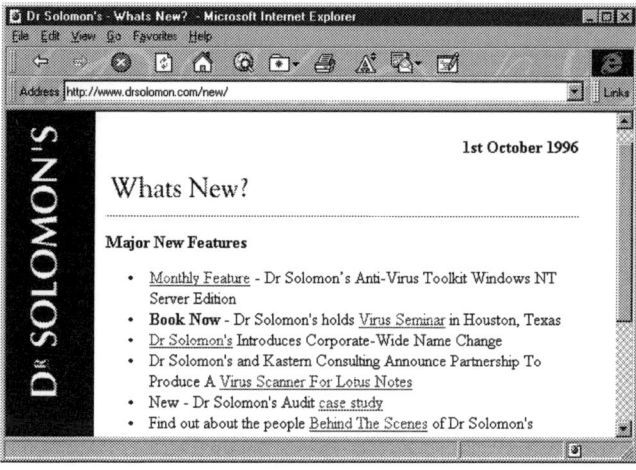

CHAPTER 11 ▽ You want software?

McAfee VirusScan – http://www.mcafee.com
Regular updates, large user base.

Norton AntiVirus – http://www.symantec.com

3. *You get what you pay for.* The software you find might be very good – some, like Paintshop Pro and PC Write are excellent. But often the package is the result of work done in someone's spare time, so don't expect miracles.

4. *You've only done half the job.* When you get the software to your computer, you still have to install it. Sometimes this can be the biggest part of the job, and free software doesn't have a handy helpline to call if you get stuck. Don't panic though – you're on e-mail, and there's usually someone you can contact if it doesn't work. The answer might take a day or two, but it should come.

Some FTP Sites to Get you Started

CU-SeeMe
ftp://gated.cornell.edu/pub/video/
Internet video conferencing? Proof that the video telephone has a long way to go.

F-Prot
ftp://risc.ua.edu/pub/ibm-antivirus/
A basic anti-virus program.

HotDog
ftp://ftp.sausage.com/pub
Automatically generates Web pages. Has a lot of fans, and a sense of humour.

VMPeg
ftp://papa.indstate.edu/winsock~1/Windows95/Graphics
Video player for your PC.

CHAPTER 12

You can broadcast too

Many people think the Internet is like a giant television network, sending information on thousands of channels direct to your computer. All you have to do is turn on, and tune in.

But that is only half the story.

The glory of the Internet is that it makes you into a broadcaster or a publisher too. You don't need to pay printers or own a television station. You already have everything you need – namely, a computer, a modem and an Internet connection.

Many Net users would go further and tell you that it is your responsibility to get involved. As a self-regulating community,

CHAPTER 12 ▽ You can broadcast too

the Internet relies on its members to provide content. That is, after all, how the Internet developed, rather than waiting for a company like the BBC to launch a service and then develop the Internet as a way of distributing it.

So throw off your inhibitions. Become a couch commando rather than a couch potato. If you don't find what you want on the Internet, don't sit there and complain about it, do something. It's the Internet way.

We'll take a look at all the ways you can contribute to the Internet. In the next chapter, we'll give you a brief introduction to creating your home page on the World Wide Web. But first, let's start on the beginner slopes.

E-mail

Of course e-mail demands a certain effort, because you have to type the text, find who to send it to, and then send the message. But that is hardly broadcasting – unless you decide to send your message to more than one person.

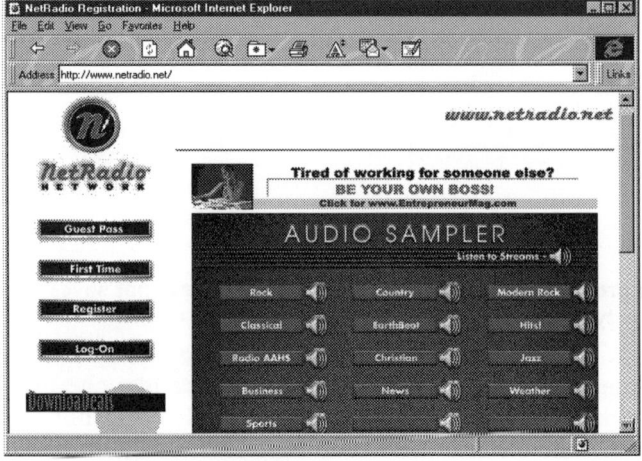

You'll find some serious broadcasting going on at NetRadio (http://www.netradio.net)

Many users organize themselves into informal groups of Net users who share a common interest. For example, if you and half a dozen friends share a fascination for light bulb jokes, and Alex hears a good one, he knows to send it as a message to Bill. Bill adds a comment, and passes it on to Chris, who knows to pass it on to Dave, and so on. The message literally circles the globe, gaining comments as it travels. By the time the message reaches Alex again, it will probably contain a number of related jokes and comments.

The problem with this approach is that it gets cumbersome – half a dozen e-mail headers, extra comments and jokes make a hefty message. Instead, you can send the e-mail to many users at once by putting all the recipient addresses together as a group in your e-mail address book.

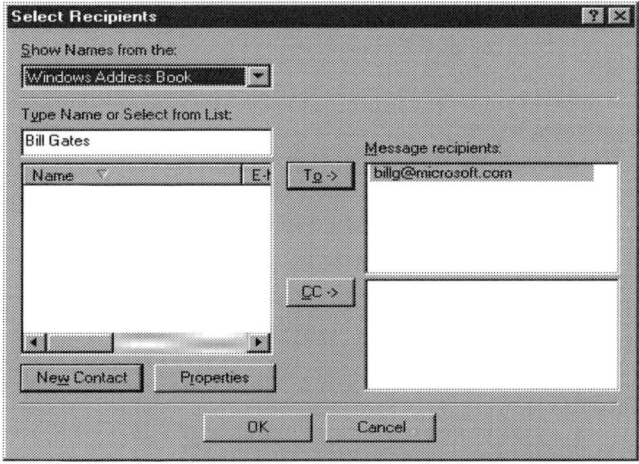

Many e-mail programs include an Address Book facility that saves you having to type those weird addresses yourself

Then each message gets posted to everyone. This is more efficient (sending the same message to 12 people costs not much more in time on line than sending one message to one person) but has limited opportunity to comment to other people's messages. But the Internet finds a way to solve this.

CHAPTER 12 ▽ You can broadcast too

Mailing Lists

A mailing list is an informal club (the Internet has few formal clubs) of people with a common interest. There are thousands of them, with every interest imaginable covered. Unfortunately there is not yet one for light bulb jokes (although there are many Web pages for them, including one that displays a different joke every 10 seconds).

To find a mailing list, either join news.lists on Usenet (see Chapter 7 if you have forgotten how) or go to the Web page `http://catalog.com/vivian/interest-group-search.html`, where you can search for a mailing list group on your chosen subject.

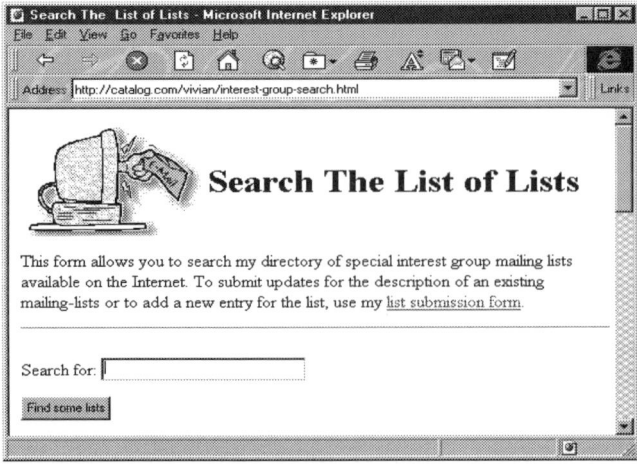

The List of Lists can lead you to mailing lists covering any subject you'd care to mention (and many more you wouldn't!)

When you subscribe to a mailing list, you will get a regular e-mail made up of postings to that list. Depending on how popular the list is, this can happen every day or only every few months – some heavy-traffic groups post more than once a day! When you read the messages, if there is something

▽ **Mailing Lists**

you want to add, you normally e-mail your contribution to the list administrator, who weeds out the junk and compiles a new posting.

This is the form for moderated lists, and because of this most have an extremely high proportion of useful information.

Joining a Mailing List

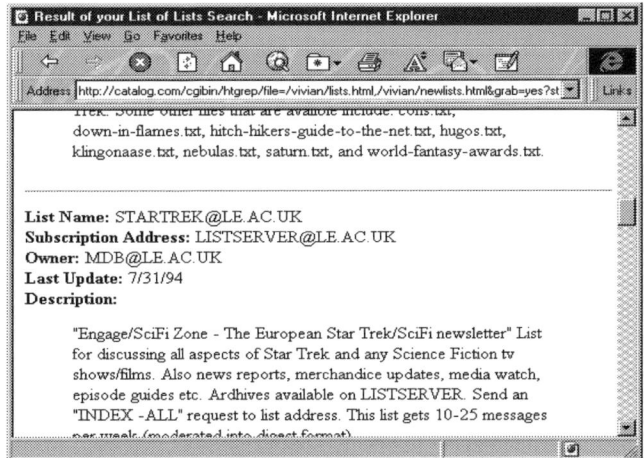

Search results from The List of Lists with descriptions and details on how to subscribe to your chosen list

Every list has a name, an address and an owner. As you can see above, the European *Star Trek* newsletter is based at Listserver@le.ac.uk, and is called STARTREK. The @le.ac.uk tells you the rest of the group's e-mail address for submissions to the group.

To suscribe, you simply send a mail message to the list's subscription address – not to the list – with the subject:

    SUBSCRIBE <list name> <your first name>

        <your second name>

the body of the e-mail address doesn't matter. To subscribe to this list, send a message to Listserver@le.ac.uk with the subject:

        SUBSCRIBE startrek John Smith

Note: Sometimes, you find yourself deluged by messages. If the volume of postings gets too much, then send a message to the same site with the subject:

        SIGNOFF startrek

Mailing lists are the great information bargains of the Internet. Go ahead and join one, or two, or three.

Newsgroups

Browsing through newsgroups is a fine way to make the time pass and the telephone bill soar. Sooner or later, though, you will see someone asking a question that you can answer, or expressing an opinion that you feel drawn to comment on. At this point you either shut up and hope someone else comments for you – you become, in Internet parlance, a 'lurker' – or you get stuck in and comment. We covered commenting to a test newsgroup in Chapter 7, but that's just playing. Now is your chance to be a responsible Internet citizen.

Contributing to a newsgroup could not be easier. In your newsgroups window, hit the button that says 'Reply to Group'. Up pops a window with the list of groups that your reply will be posted in, and the opportunity to send a carbon copy to anyone in your address book. Type the message, click 'post message', and off it goes.

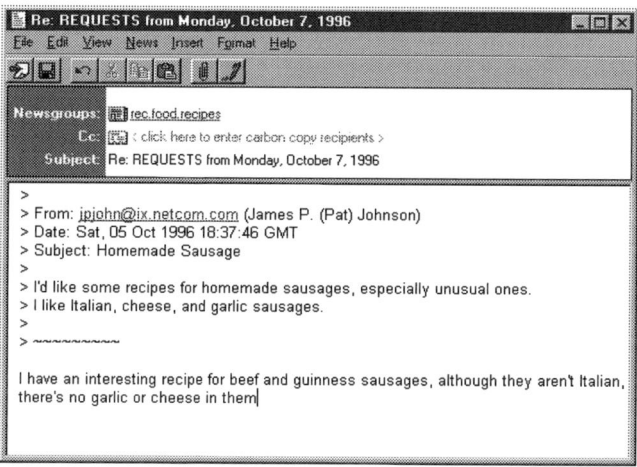

Click 'Reply to Group', type your message, and click the first toolbar button to send it

If you want a more private conversation, click on 'Reply to Author', to send a private mail message to the original poster. Be careful not to confuse these two if the information is sensitive – one person can read a private message. Forty million people can read one posted to a newsgroup.

The etiquette of posting to a newsgroup is part of the next chapter, but if you don't want to read that, then there are three things to remember: quote the original message when you reply (your browser quotes the original message automatically), be concise, and don't comment unless you have something to say.

IRC

As you have already heard, Internet Relay Chat is the citizen's band of the Internet. Some pretty wild conversations happen out there on IRC, so it is not a cool place to dump the kids while you are out at the shops.

CHAPTER 12 ▽ You can broadcast too

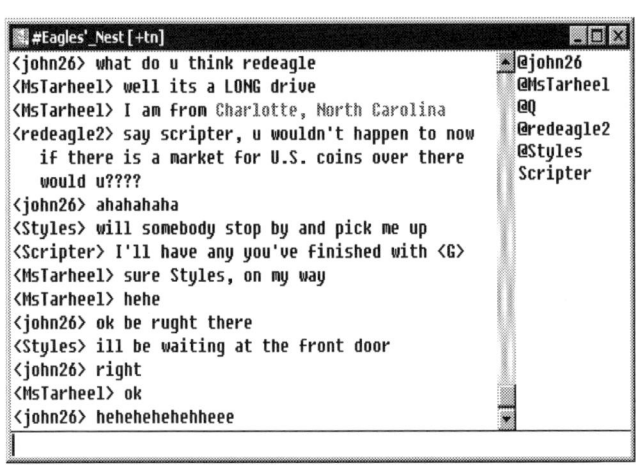

The wit, wisdom, and incisive topical debate of an IRC session

Everything on IRC happens in real time. This means that as you type the message on your keyboard, it appears on the screen of everyone else logged into your IRC session. This makes viewing an IRC session like listening to a crowded room where everyone is shouting at once. It is either exhilarating, or it gives you a headache.

Some ISPs provide a dedicated IRC program, others don't. For example, BTInternet users call up the BTInternet dialler, and click on 'chat with others'. Other users will have to download a free IRC client. Try ftp://papa.indstate.edu/winsock~1/winirc/ for one called WS IRC – the standard for Net users.

IRC is hard to get used to: it is literally a world of its own. Also, you are not anonymous, and everyone else in the session knows you are there. There's not the space to give you a full lesson in IRC here, but use your hard-won FTP expertise to pick up a free primer from ftp://ftp.cs.bu.edu/irc/support/.

Your ISP will tell you its local IRC server. Your software has a setup box in which you enter it, then when you're set up, dial up the Internet and log in.

IRC has its own language, and it's nothing like as easy as sending e-mail, or writing a Web page. When your IRC software shows you are connected, type /LIST, and you get a list of the current channels that are available.

Channels are the different 'conversations' on IRC. They all begin with '#'. When you select one (type /JOIN [channel name]), you'll plunge in, and your presence will be announced to everyone else there. At this point, it's polite to say hello, as if you had just sidled up to a conversation.

The commands you'll need regularly are:

/WHO*   which tells you the nicknames of who else is there
/MSG [nickname]   which sends a private message to someone
/LEAVE [channel]   exits that particular conversation

and essential to know:

/HELP   which gives you a list of commands, and
/BYE   which gets you out of IRC quick

IRC etiquette is not complicated: anything goes. But if you are deliberately annoying or anti-social, you will find that being on line makes people feel free to be as rude as they like to you. Also you will need to mug up on your acronyms, so revise Chapter 15 before attempting a serious IRC chat.

Remember that the personal details an IRC user gives are not necessarily true. Here's the oldest Internet joke: On The Net, Nobody Knows You Are A Dog. Nobody knows whether you are a man or a woman, old or young, rich or poor. This can be tremendously liberating – but be careful when divulging personal information to someone you don't know anything about.

IRC is addictive. It is full of students, some who spend the entire day talking on IRC in their computer science

CHAPTER 12 ▽ **You can broadcast too**

department because they don't have to pay the phone bill, unlike you. It is also a great way to make friends and find support, advice or sympathy.

Internet Telephony and Videoconferencing

The Internet has the advantage that wherever you call, you only pay for the call costs of a local telephone conversation. Not surprisingly, some bright sparks have brought out 'Internet phones' which turn your Internet connection into a telephone connection.

The free Net2Phone utility: download it from http://www.net2phone.com, buy a microphone and soundcard, and start saving a fortune!

The result: a call to Australia costs the same as a local call.

This is emerging technology, so let's stick it in the 'too good to be true' basket for now. The conversations are not 'full

▽ Internet Telephony and Videoconferencing   129

duplex', that means that only one person can talk at one time, like a walkie-talkie. And there's the small matter that Internet service providers are legally not supposed to use the Net for transmitting voice.

Eventually it seems likely that the Internet phone will become easier to use, legal, and save us all a mint. At that time, we'll also be able to broadcast pictures. There's some software called CU-SeeMe which does this over the Internet already, but try doing this down an Internet phone line, and you can see how far away the videophone still is.

CHAPTER 13

Making your own page

You have seen the Web pages that other people, companies and organizations put up. It's quite likely that you have seen a couple that make you think 'I'd like to do that'. Well, you can. One of the remarkable things about the World Wide Web is that you don't need thousands of pounds and a degree in computer science to put up a Web page.

What Do I Do?

Briefly, you write the text and find the images you want to put up on your Web pages. You design how they will look and how you get from one to the other, and write commands into the text so that a computer displaying the page knows how to organize it. You then copy all the computer files you have written or scanned into a directory on your service provider's Internet server.

▽ **What Do I Put on My Pages?**

Not everyone with an Internet account can do this – you need your service provider to offer you space on the server for your files. BTInternet offers 5 Mb of free space for its users, which is plenty of room for an all-singing, all-dancing personal page.

What Do I Put on My Pages?

Good question. And to judge by the appearance of some home pages, not always a question that Internet users have a good answer for. To be honest, it doesn't matter what you put on your page, as long as you bear in mind that it is being viewed by people of all ages and in many countries – try to consider what they may find offensive, even if you don't. No one minds if your Web page isn't the most profound document since the Domesday Book.

The most basic home page tells the visitor about yourself. Try writing 500 words about yourself and you will cover your interests, your hobbies, and all sorts of other material that can be used as a source of links – jumps to other pages, either written by yourself or other people, dealing with that subject.

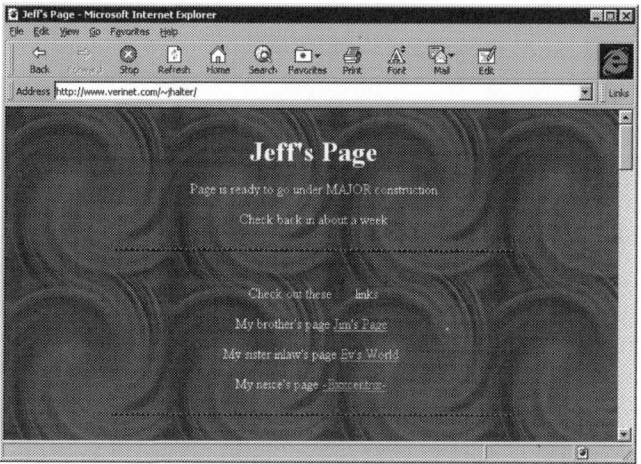

Begin with a simple page containing a few links and add some fancier details as you learn more

CHAPTER 13 ▽ Making your own page

For example, if you write on your home page that your favourite sport is judo, supply a link to a favourite judo site that you visit. This means that the person reading about you can begin to share your interests. It also means that you don't have to write pages explaining judo – unless you want to.

Other ideas for pages could include:

- A noticeboard for a club or society
- A CV or résumé
- A list of your favourite sites
- A page to advertise some product or service that you sell.

Or, of course, your site can be all of the above. The only limitation is your imagination.

How Do Web Pages Work?

Next time you are browsing the Web, go to a page you like. Pull down the File menu in your browser and save the page to your hard disk under a name like 'stuff.htm'. Make the last letters of the name '.htm'. When you have logged off, find the file and open it – the browser starts up again, and you will see the page – though without pictures or fancy graphics. Close the browser.

Now start up your basic text editor (Notepad for Windows users) and open the same file from the text editor. You should see the same text, but with a bunch of additions in brackets, as shown overleaf.

▽ **Introducing HTML**

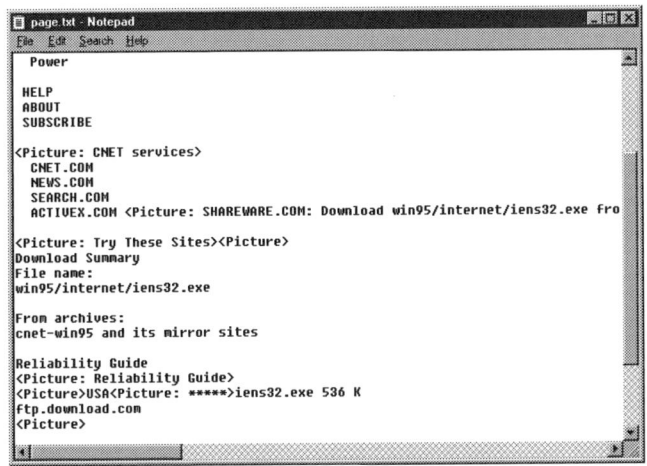

Plain text, with the extra bracketed bits that make it a Web page

The bits in brackets (⟨bits⟩) are the instructions to tell your computer how a page should be displayed. They are called HyperText Markup Language, although everyone calls it HTML for short. HTML looks like gobbledegook, but you can learn the basics in a couple of hours.

Introducing HTML

So what's HyperText Markup Language all about? Well, we've met hypertext already – those underlined, clickable links that make the Web so easy to navigate. A *markup language* is a set of codes or signs added to plain text to indicate how it should be presented to the reader, noting bold or italic text, paragraph breaks, and so on. When you type any document into your word-processor, it adds these codes for you, but tactfully hides them from view: if you wanted bold text, for example, it *shows* you bold text instead of those codes. In HTML, however, you have to type in the codes yourself along with the text, and your browser puts the whole lot together before displaying it.

CHAPTER 13 ▽ Making your own page

These codes are known as **tags**, and they consist of ordinary text placed between less-than and greater-than signs. Let's take an example:

```
<B>Welcome to my homepage.</B>
Glad you could make it!
```

The first tag, <B>, means 'turn on bold type'. Halfway through the line, the same tag is used again, but with a forward-slash inserted straight after the less-than sign: this means 'turn off bold type'. If you displayed a page containing this line in your browser, it would look like this:

Welcome to my homepage. Glad you could make it!

Of course, there's more to a Web page than bold text, so clearly there must be many more of these tags. But don't let that worry you – you don't have to learn all of them! There's a small bundle that you'll use a lot, and you'll get to know those very quickly. Others will begin to sink in once you've used them a few times.

Getting Started with HTML

There are a few bits and pieces that will appear in almost every HTML document you write, so let's start by making a template file you can use every time you want to create a new page. Start Notepad, and type the text below (without worrying about the exact number of spaces or carriage returns). Save this file using any name you like, but make sure you give it the extension **.htm** or **.html**. Every Web page you write must be saved with one of these extensions – it doesn't matter which you choose, but you'll find life a lot easier if you stick to the same one each time!

```
<!DOCTYPE HTML PUBLIC ''-//W3C//DTD HTML
3.2//EN''>
```

▽ **Add A Title and Text**

```
<HTML>
<HEAD>
    <TITLE>Untitled</TITLE>
</HEAD>

<BODY>


</BODY>
</HTML>
```

None of these tags does anything exciting by itself, but it's worth knowing what they're all for. The first line is a piece of technical nonsense that tells a browser that the document is written in the latest version of the HTML language. The rest of the document is placed between the <HTML> and </HTML> tags, and falls into two separate chunks: the **head** (the section between <HEAD> and </HEAD>) and the **body** (between <BODY> and </BODY>).

The document's head is pretty dull: all it contains is the title of the document, inserted between the <TITLE> and </TITLE> tags. The body section is the one that matters. Between these two tags you'll type all the text that should appear on your page, and put in the tags you need to display images, set colours, insert links to other pages and sites, and anything else you want your page to contain.

Now that you've created a basic template, let's start adding to it to build up a respectable-looking page.

Add A Title and Text

The first thing to do is to replace the word **Untitled** with a sensible title for the page, such as **Links To The Best Multimedia Sites** or **My EastEnders HomePage**. Pick something that describes what the page will be about, but

CHAPTER 13 ▽ Making your own page

keep it fairly short: the text between the <TITLE> and </TITLE> tags will appear in the title-bar at the very top of most browsers, and if you're entry is too long to fit, it'll just get chopped off!

Now we'll add some text to the page. Either type the same as I've entered below, or replace my first and second paragraph entries with whole paragraphs if you prefer. When you've done that, save the file as **links.htm** or **links.html**, but don't close Notepad yet.

```
<!DOCTYPE HTML PUBLIC ''-//W3C//DTD HTML 3.2//EN''>


<HTML>
<HEAD>
     <TITLE>Links To The Best Multimedia
     Sites</TITLE>
</HEAD>


<BODY>
<H1>Welcome To My Homepage!</H1>
Here's the first paragraph.
<P>And here's the second paragraph.


</BODY>
</HTML>
```

Now take a look at your masterpiece in your browser. There are several ways you can do this: find the file you just saved and double-click it, or open your browser and choose **File | Open** and then click on **Browse**. When your browser displays it, it should look a lot like the next figure.

▽ **Add A Title and Text** 137

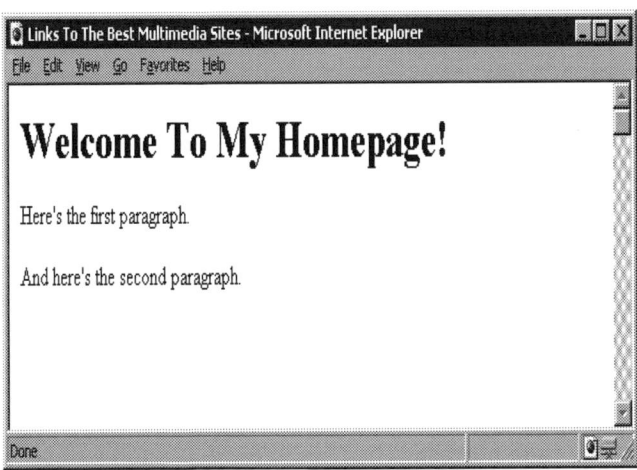

So what are those new tags all about? Let's take the `<P>` tag first. This tells your browser to present the following text as a new paragraph, which automatically inserts a blank line before it. And this raises an important point about HTML: you can't insert blank lines just by pressing Enter or Return. Although *you* can see blank lines in Notepad when you do that, your browser will just ignore them, which is why you need to start a new paragraph by entering `<P>` (Notice that you don't have to put in a closing `</P>` at the end of a paragraph – the act of starting a new paragraph isn't an ongoing effect that has to be turned off again). You can also start a new line *without* starting a new paragraph by inserting a single `<BR>` tag where you want the line-break to occur.

The other pair of tags that cropped up was `<H1>` and `</H1>` which format a line of text as a heading. You can choose from six sizes: H1 is the largest, followed by `<H2>` and `</H2>` down to the smallest, `<H6>` and `</H6>`. In one nifty little manoeuvre, these tags change the size of the text you place between them *and* make it bold. They also automatically start a new paragraph for the heading (so you don't need to place a `<P>` tag at the start of the line) and start a new paragraph for whatever follows the heading. Try changing the size of the heading by altering those tags to see the different effects, re-saving the file, and clicking your browser's **Refresh** button to update it.

Be Bold. (Or Be Italic . . .)

The tags for bold and italic text are easy to remember: `<B>` for bold, and `<I>` for italic. As both of these are ongoing effects, you'll have to enter closing tags (`</B>` or `</I>`) when you want the effect to stop. And, just as in your word-processor, you can combine these tags, so if your document contained this:

This is `<I>`italic`</I>`. This is `<B>`bold`</B>`. This is `<B><I>`bold & italic`</I></B>`.

the result would look like this in your browser:

This is *italic*. This is **bold**. This is ***bold & italic.***

Lesser-used text formatting tags that might come in handy one day are superscript (`<SUP>` and `</SUP>`) and subscript (`<SUB>` and `</SUB>`). If you really feel the urge, you can underline text using another memorable pair of tags, `<U>` and `</U>`, but be careful how you use underlining: most people surfing the Web expect underlined text to be a hyperlink, and might find your gratuitous use of these tags confusing.

Insert Links To Other Sites

It's an unwritten rule of the Internet that a Web site should contain links to *other* Web sites. After all, the entire Web works by being inter-connected, and if people surf their way to your site and have to retrace their steps before they can

▽ Insert Links To Other Sites

continue surfing, they'll steer clear in future! So let's put in another <P> tag to start a new paragraph, and add that sorely-needed link as shown below:

<P>Visit Macromedia's snazzy <A HREF=''http://www.macromedia.com/shockzone''> Shockzone</A> site.

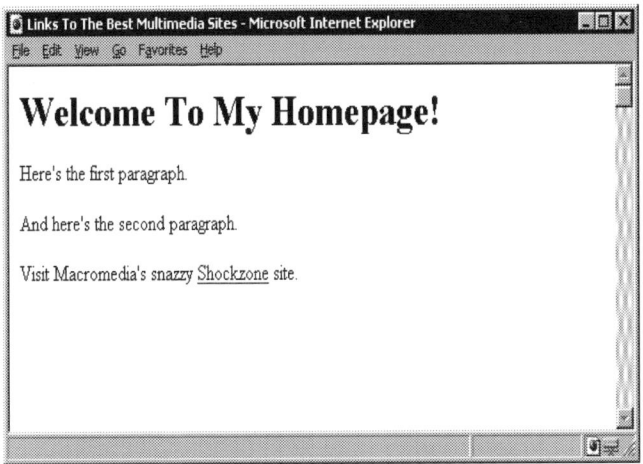

This is a more complicated tag, so let's look at it bit by bit. Although we call these 'links', in HTML they're called anchors, and that's where the A comes from after the first < sign. An anchor usually begins with the <A HREF= tag. Following that comes the URL of the page you want to link to, always enclosed in double-quotes, and the > sign to finish the opening anchor tag.

Immediately after the opening anchor tag, type the text you want visitors to your page to click on. This might be a single word, a sentence, or even a whole paragraph, but don't forget to put *something* here, or there'll be nothing to click on to reach that site! Finally, type the closing anchor tag, </A>.

CHAPTER 13 ▽ Making your own page

Links To Pages On Your Own Site

The link we just added used something called an **absolute URL**. In fact, that's the only type of URL you've seen so far: an absolute URL gives the whole path to the page you want to open, including the http:// bit and the name of the computer. When you want to create links to other pages on your *own* site you can use a different, simpler method.

Using the template we made earlier, create a new HTML document, and save it to the directory where the other is stored. Let's assume you've called it **morelinks.html**. Now, in your first document, you can create a link to this new page by typing this anchor:

<A HREF=''morelinks.html''>Here's a few more links.</A>

Yes, it's just a filename. This is called a **relative URL**. It tells your browser to look for a file called **morelinks.html** and display it. Since a browser doesn't know where else to look, it searches the directory containing the document it's displaying at that moment. As long as **morelinks.html** really is in that same directory, the browser will find it and open it.

So what's so great about relative URLs? First, less typing. That also lessens the chances of mistakes. But best of all, you can click these links in your browser to check that they work. If you click a link to an absolute URL, your browser will have to dial up and connect to that computer first.

You can make a browser look somewhere different for a file in a similar way. Open the directory containing these two documents, create a subdirectory called **pages**, and move the **morelinks.html** file into it. The link we just added now needs to be changed to the following:

<A HREF="pages/morelinks.html">Here's a few more links.</A>

▽ **Let's Get Colourful!**

The browser now looks in the current directory for another directory called **pages**, and looks inside that for **morelinks.html**.

Finally, let's open **morelinks.html** and create a link back to our original document (which we called **links.html**) so that you can click your way to and fro between the two. To do this, we need to tell the browser to look in the parent directory of **pages** to find this file. If you're familiar with using MS-DOS, you'll recognize this straight away: to move up one level in the directory tree, just type two dots:

```
<A HREF=''../links.html''>Here's my first links page.</A>
```

So far we've looked at linking to other Web pages, but a link needn't necessarily point to a **.html** document. If you have a movie file, a text file, a sound file, or whatever, create the link in exactly the same way entering the location and name of this file between the double-quotes. If the file is particularly large, though, it's good practice to mention its size somewhere nearby so that people can choose whether or not to click that link.

Let's Get Colourful!

So far, in our example Web page, everything looks a bit dull. The background is white, the text is black, the links are blue – these are the default colours set up by Internet Explorer, and it's using them because we haven't told it to use anything different. All of this is easily changed, though, by typing our preferences into that opening <BODY> tag.

This brings us to a new area of HTML. A tag like <B> is self-contained – it simply turns on bold text, with no complications. Other tags need to contain a little more information about what you want to do. This is done by adding extra pieces of text to a tag, each separated by a

CHAPTER 13 ▽ Making your own page

space, and these extra bits are called **attributes**. They usually consist of the setting's name, an equals sign, and the setting you want to make, such as BGCOLOR=blue.

The <BODY> tag doesn't *have* to contain attributes, but browsers will use their own default settings for anything you haven't specified, and different browsers use different defaults. Most Web authors like to keep as much control as possible over how their pages will be displayed, and make their own settings for the body attributes. Here are 6 attributes you can use in the <BODY> tag:

This attribute...	...has this effect
BGCOLOR=	Sets the background colour of the Web page
TEXT=	Sets the colour of text on the page
LINK=	Sets the colour of the clickable hyperlinks
VLINK=	Sets the colour of a link to a previously-visited page
ALINK=	Sets the colour of a link between the time it's clicked and the new page opening

Without further ado, open the original **links.html** document you created in the last chapter, and change the <BODY> tag so that it looks like this:

<BODY BGCOLOR=MAROON TEXT=WHITE LINK=YELLOW VLINK=OLIVE ALINK=LIME>

Save the file, and take a look at it in your browser. Okay, the colour scheme may not be to your taste, but it's starting to resemble a 'real' Web page! Try swapping colours around to find a scheme you prefer. There are 140 colours to choose from. We don't have space to list them all here, but they include standard colour-names like red, orange, purple, black, navy and blue.

A Few HTML Tips

Of course this can't be an exhaustive guide to HTML, but you should be off to a flying start. There are many guides and tutorials on the Web itself which can help you improve your skills, and you'll find two of the best at:

    http://www.asiweb.com/htmlauth.htm.
    http://www.ncsa.uiuc.edu/General/Internet/WWW/
    HTMLPrimer.html

To round off this first look at HTML, here's a few quick tips worth keeping in mind:

- Browsers treat spaces in almost the same way they treat carriage returns: only the first space you type will be observed, so a row of spaces in Notepad will appear as a single space on the web page.
- All the file names you refer to are case-sensitive. If you try to link to a page called rocket.htm and that page is actually called Rocket.htm, the browser will display an error instead.
- You can centre text (or anything else) on the page by enclosing it between <CENTER> and </CENTER> tags (but note the American spelling!). This might be just a single word, an image, or the entire contents of your page-body.
- You can break a page into 'sections' by placing a horizontal line across the page. Just insert the tag <HR> where you want the line to appear. It will automatically be placed on a new line with a paragraph break above and below it.

Short Cuts

If learning HTML seems like too much effort, the good news is, you might not have to. If you have a word processor, then you will be able to get an extra piece of software to allow you to save your documents as HTML files: Word, WordPerfect and Word Pro all supply this either in the box, or as a free download. This works, but you may be disappointed by the result. HTML cannot cope with fancy word-processor fonts, so the page will be much plainer than you thought.

Another much-used short cut is to find a page you like, save it to your hard disk, then replace all the text with your own text. This is not recommended if the site in question contains copyright material. Contrary to what you often hear, copyright laws apply just as much on the Internet as anywhere else.

Finally, there are some dedicated HTML production tools which are useful if you are making a lot of pages. A shareware tool called HTML Pro (find your local download site from http://www.shareware.com) has a lot of admirers; you'll also find a jokey piece of shareware called HotDog that does the same thing. There are many others, but give HTML a go before you splash out. Software might help, but practice helps more.

Five Don'ts and Five Do's for Web Pages

DON'T worry if you think your page isn't important enough. This is the magazine about yourself you always wanted to publish. Enjoy the limelight.

DO have a go. Half the Internet is a work in progress. There's no need to be perfect before you put up a page.

▽ Five Don'ts and Five Do's for Web Pages   145

DON'T rip off copyright material! You can put a link to a site in your page, but don't copy from that site without the author's permission.

DO trawl other sites for ideas. Seeing how others design their pages is a big help.

DON'T get carried away with colours and flashy design! Some sites are queasy with flashing purple text on a green striped background. More people will visit a site that is easy to read.

DO break your site down into lots of pages with short sections of text. It is hard to read on a screen which contains only a few hundred words. If you break your text up into chunks, you can have a front page, like a contents page, that allows you to jump to each 'chunk' in turn.

DON'T get discouraged if it seems difficult at first. Keep your site simple – you can add to it tomorrow, next week or next year. Check your HTML carefully for errors, as it needs to be exectly right to work.

DO try to incorporate pictures into your page. If you have a photograph, some photocopy shops will be able to turn it into a computer file for you.

DON'T worry about breaking your computer and don't think that everyone is watching you struggle. They aren't. If you ask other users to visit your site and make suggestions, most will be interested and positive.

DO tell people who might be interested that your site is there. Send mail messages to the online search engines to tell them you exist!

CHAPTER 14

Netiquette for beginners

If you read nothing else before going on line, read this chapter! It's short, there's not much jargon, and it could save you from a grisly experience.

The Internet doesn't have regulations about what you can and cannot do, but it does have a code of conduct, known as netiquette. This is enforced with glee by the police of the Internet – its users. They value the Internet's independence and lack of government control, and are prepared fight to keep things that way. This means that new users occasionally suffer embarrassment as they are 'flamed' – criticized in blunt language – by fellow users for doing something inappropriate. It happens to us all; but you can avoid most of the easy mistakes.

Netiquette may seem rather old-fashioned, but it is extremely useful. When you communicate by talking face-to-face, your tone of voice and expressions express as much as the words you say. It is obvious who you are talking to, and usually those people know something about you.

▽ Basic Netiquette   147

When you communicate on the Internet, there are only the words you type. People cannot see you and probably do not know you. You are talking to a much bigger audience than usual. There are plenty of arguments on the Internet already. Without netiquette, there wouldn't be anything but people fighting.

Basic Netiquette

Newsgroups

1. NEVER TYPE IN CAPITALS ON THE INTERNET, whether you are sending e-mail or commenting in a newsgroup. Why? BECAUSE IT MAKES IT SEEM LIKE YOU ARE SHOUTING and it gives other users a headache.
2. Take time to settle into a newsgroup before commenting. It is hard to judge the mood or character of your fellow netties from one message, so read for a few days before you plunge in.
3. Every few days a newsgroup will publish its 'FAQ' – the 'Frequently asked questions'. Try and get hold of this before you start asking basic questions, because it will contain all the most common queries from new joiners like yourself. If it has not popped up in a week, then it is fine to post a message asking for the FAQ.
4. When commenting on a message, always quote the relevant text you are commenting on. Messages on Usenet become jumbled and, unless you quote, no one will know whose message you are commenting on.
5. Be concise, and make sure you have something to say. Flamers will jump on you if you quote a 200-line message in full and add 'I agree completely' at the bottom.
6. Remember not everyone knows you, so reread your messages before you post them. Did you say exactly what you meant to say?
7. Bear in mind who will read your messages – everybody. So do not be gratuitously offensive to any nationality or belief, or you will most certainly regret it. A common mistake that British people make is to poke fun at the US on line. This does not go down well with the majority of

CHAPTER 14 ▽ Netiquette for beginners

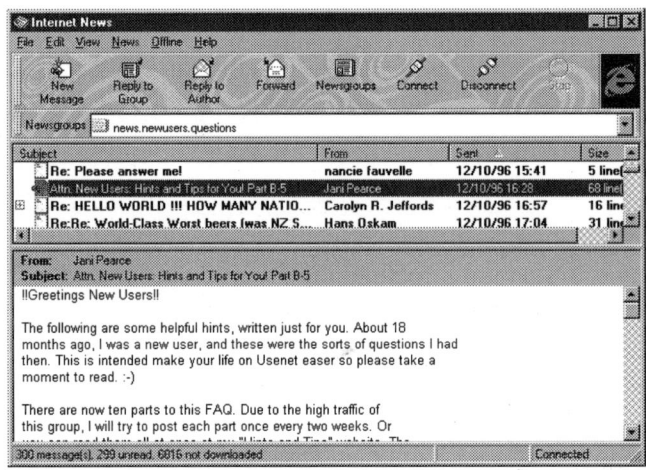

Visit **news.newusers.questions** for more useful advice than you can shake a stick at

Usenet users, who happen to live there.

8. Attach a 'sig' – a line or two about who you are, and some essential detail like your job or your home town. It helps people recognize your messages. The temptation is to expand the sig into a mini-CV, with song lyrics, pithy quotes and little pictures of yourself made by typing letters on the keyboard. Resist this temptation.

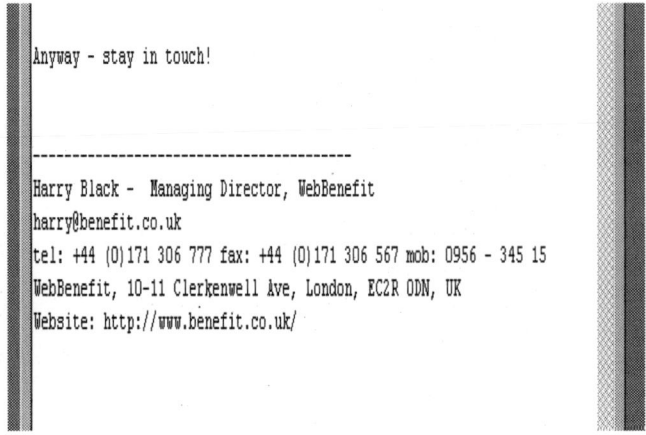

A 'sig' or signature of some sort is almost obligatory – but keep it short!

Basic Netiquette

E-mail Netiquette

1. When you get a message, reply promptly, if only to say, 'I'll get back to you'. When you send e-mail on the Net, this is the only way you will know that it has arrived!
2. Be precise when you reply. If someone raises four points in an e-mail, deal with all of them in turn.
3. Quote from the e-mail message when replying to specific points.
4. Have fun, but be brief. Don't send an essay when a paragraph will do.
5. As on Usenet, attach a sig, and – as on Usenet – keep it short.

A Word about Spam

'Spamming' is the ultimate no-no on the Internet. Spam and you will be flamed mercilessly by many rude people.

Spamming means duplicating a message to hundreds or thousands of people or newsgroups when it's irrelevant to most of them. It is Internet junk mail, and very irritating. After a few weeks on the Net, one day you will get some e-mail with a title like 'Make $$$ in three easy steps'. This will be the first of many similar spams. What's annoying is that you pay to download this message.

Spams also pop up in Usenet, sometimes because someone is trying to sell something and sometimes out of sheer laziness. Not long ago a firm of American lawyers effectively spammed the entire Usenet with one posting, almost bringing the net to its knees. If you are looking for, say, the name of a particular TV programme, only ask for it in one or two relevant groups; otherwise, people who don't know what you are talking about will see the same message 40 times.

Sometimes you commit a similar error without realizing it. If someone spams hundreds of newsgroups, it is tempting to flame them. Do it by e-mail – if you reply to the message, you'll be spamming the same newsgroups!

Smileys, Abbreviations and the World of Emoticons

That's the easy part dealt with. The other part of netiquette is the strange and wonderful language used to express yourself on the Net.

First we have acronyms – shorthand ways to express yourself that pepper mail and Usenet messages. It looks like they are designed to keep new users out, but they have a function too – they make messages shorter, and quicker to type.

Imagine you are disagreeing with someone on line. In RL (that's the acronym for real life, believe it or not) you would say 'That's not true!'. If you begin your message like that, you will only start a flame war, because in print it looks much more abrupt. So start your message 'IMHO that's not true'. IMHO means 'In my humble opinion'. Your opinion may not be humble at all, but it's a shorthand for 'I am expressing what I think here'.

Acronyms range for the simple and useful to the daft and obscure. Here are some of the more common ones:

ROFL	Rolls on floor laughing – your joke was funny
IMHO	In my humble opinion
BTDTGTTS	Been there, done that, got the t-shirt – your comment told me nothing I didn't already know
BFN	Bye for now
OIC	Oh, I see
GAL	Get a life!
TIA	Thanks in advance – used when requesting information

IYSWIM	If you see what I mean
HTH	Hope this helps
LOL	Laughed out loud – more humour approval
YHM	You have mail – I have sent you some more information, or am continuing this discussion in private
BTW	By the way

Smileys

Known to internet academics as emoticons, smileys are a way of expressing emotion in your messages. For example, someone you like gets bad news. You leave a message with 'I'm sorry to hear that,' and it sounds a bit bland. Instead

> I'm sorry to hear that :-(

uses an unhappy face (tip your head to the left to see it) to express your sympathy. If you didn't like the person,

> I'm sorry to hear that :-)

expresses lack of sympathy.

Always try to use smileys when a comment can express different emotions. but don't overuse them or it makes your message difficult to read. More than two in a message is usually too many.

A note on humour: the British sense of humour does not travel well on line. Sarcasm and irony can sometimes sound like rudeness in San Francisco or Singapore, so remember your smileys when you make fun of people!

CHAPTER 14 ▽ Netiquette for beginners

A Small Dictionary of Smileys

:-)	happy
:-(	sad
:-D	laughing
=:-(	frown
:-0	shock! horror! surprise!
;-)	nudge, nudge, wink, wink
8-)	smiley wearing glasses
:-)=	smiley with a beard
:-X	I'll say nothing (mouth taped up)
:-P	yah boo (sticking out tongue)
:-*	kiss

CHAPTER 15

Net myths and reality

You've read it in the papers, you've seen it on TV – the Internet is awash with pornography, recipes for bombs and hackers who steal your credit card number. It is also the global information superhighway which will replace shops, banks and even the pub. We'll all be using mini-computers this time next year which fit in your top pocket and cost less than a packet of cigarettes.

Some of this is true, a lot of it is rubbish. Let's separate the fact from the fiction.

Are There Really No Laws on the Internet?

This is a myth, propagated by scaremongers who haven't read their law books. The Internet causes existing laws a lot of problems, but the forces of law and order are just beginning to catch up with the potential for criminal use of the Net – and are finding that existing laws are completely sufficient to prosecute offenders.

The problem is that the Internet makes distribution of information easy. So if someone wants to send child pornography across the world, Customs and Excise cannot stop it if that person sends it on the Internet. However, possession of child pornography is still an offence, whether that material is on paper or is a computer file – and there have been prosecutions for possession of images stored on a computer.

You will also be breaking the law if you use copyright material without permission. That means images from someone else's Web site, text from a copyrighted essay published on line – even a distinctive design. If in doubt, check with the owner of the Web site that you can use the material.

Is the Net Full of Pornography?

No, it is not. Count the sites on the Web and the Usenet newsgroups and, by that measure, the Internet is less than 1 per cent pornography. Compare that to the composition of your local newsagent, and you find that the Internet has considerably more intellectual content.

On the other hand, that 1 per cent of the Internet is probably its most visited section. You would also have a very strong stomach not to be offended by some of the content that appears on Usenet. In an attempt to avoid government controls, the providers of hard-core pornography on the Net try to implement some sort of access controls. These are mostly voluntary, involving the user clicking on a button to declare they he or she is 18 (or 21) and unlikely to be offended. There are also several voluntary codes that register sites for content, like the ratings for cinema films.

▽ **Content Filters**

In the UK the police have a special unit looking into the spread of Internet pornography: they advise service providers if they believe certain newsgroups contain obscene material.

Obviously voluntary controls aren't much good if you want to keep your kids away from material you consider unsuitable. Instead you need software that allows selective access to the Internet.

Content Filters

If you want to control the access a member of your family has to sites containing unsuitable material, then there are plenty of methods you can use.

The most obvious are the programs called 'content filters' – pieces of software that don't allow access to certain sites. If you use a filter and try to go to the Penthouse home page for example, a message pops up instead to say that the site is barred to you.

The four most popular filters are called SurfWatch (the original filter), CyberSitter, NetNanny or CyberPatrol. All four are downloadable from the Internet – the addresses are at the end of this section. You pay for this software by subscribing for regular updates.

The people who sell the software monitor the content of the Internet, and check new sites. They compile a 'banned list' of sites, which is encrypted so that it cannot be changed by computer-savvy kids. When a child tries to go to a page on the list, the software blocks access.

The software also has a list of unsuitable words: explicit sexual swear words, violence or racism, which it checks for on all sites accessed that are not on the 'banned list'. If it encounters those words, it blocks access to the site.

CHAPTER 15 ▽ Net myths and reality

Though not perfect, the filters have worked remarkably well. Parents can customize the access, allowing kids to get to sites that they consider 'safe' but prohibited by the filter. When you subscribe, you can download regular updates to the list of banned sites.

The filters will also allow you to set time limits for browsing. That means you can relax, knowing that your kids aren't going to get 'addicted' to the Internet, and you will have a manageable phone bill.

```
CyberPatrol - http://www.microsys.com/cyber/
   default.htm
SurfWatch - http://www.surfwatch.com
```

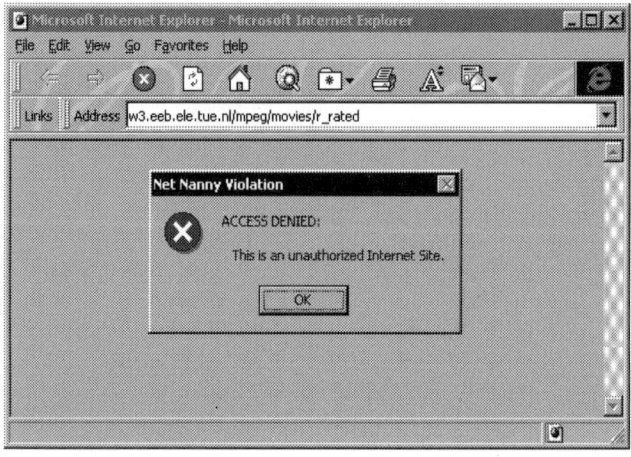

Net Nanny says 'No'

```
NetNanny - http://www.netnanny.com/netnanny
CyberSitter - http://www.solidoak.com
```

Weaker filtering is provided by the Recreational Software Advisory Council (RSAC) system of rating sites. The RSAC runs a voluntary scheme where Web site designers fill in a questionnaire about their site, and the RSAC provides a rating, like the one you get on a home video.

If you want to block access to RSAC adult-rated sites in Internet Explorer, open the View menu, select Options, and then click the Security tab. Click the button marked 'Settings ... and enter the same password into both boxes, then click OK. (Whatever you do, don't forget the password you chose! You'll need it to change the security settings in future, or to view restricted sites yourself.) This will take you to a page like the one shown in the following screenshot. On the first tab, labelled Ratings, select one of the four categories, and drag the slider to the left or right to choose the level of content you feel is suitable for users to access. For young children, for example, you may wish to leave the slider for each category fully to the left.

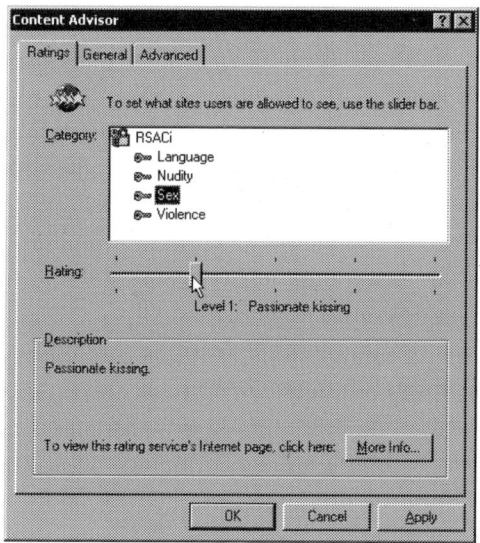

You can use Internet Explorer's built-in ratings system to control access to web sites.

Next click the General tab and you'll see two checkboxes at the top of the page. The first of these, 'Users can see sites which have no rating' is best left empty (unchecked) – this ensures that users will be barred from any site that hasn't been rated by the RSACi. You might want to check the second box, marked 'Supervisor can type a password to allow users to view restricted content'; you can then view any site, regardless of content, by typing your password when prompted. Click OK to confirm these settings, and you'll be returned to the main Security page. Click on 'Enable Ratings' and enter your password, and your security settings will take effect. Any time you want to turn them off, return to the Security page, click 'Disable Ratings' and enter your password.

Popular as the RSAC is, a small proportion of the adult sites on the Net have registered. It's no substitute for a content filter.

Content filters are half the solution. There's no substitute for being aware and informed about what your kids are doing on line. Surfing the Internet needn't be a solitary occupation – find sites they would like, and encourage them to visit sites that will help with their homework. Trust your kids, and learn about surfing the Net with them. Don't expect a content filter to be a good parent.

Can a Hacker Get Access to My Computer?

No. Your computer does not become part of the Internet. It links to a larger computer that is joined to the Internet instead, so someone else on the Net cannot peer into your computer unless you specifically invite them in.

▽ **I Can Buy Anything I Want on the Web**

The danger comes when you download software from the Net. This is usually reliable if you download from a commercial site (it's in their interest, after all), but if you get your software from a University site or a public bulletin board, you take a risk that you could download a virus. There are some anti-virus products which will act as sentries when you download software: see Chapter 11 for the details.

I'm a Woman – Will I be Sexually Harassed if I Go On Line?

There have been isolated incidents of sexual harassment on the Internet, which again paints a misleading picture. This is not to say that sexual harassment is insignificant in any form. The Internet, with its heavy male bias (some surveys have males outnumbering females by four to one) has some nutters who think constant sexual innuendo is funny. Often this is jumped on by irate fellow Internet users. If you are harassed by e-mail, then a complaint to the administrator of the abuser's service provider is usually sufficient to get him kicked off the service. And don't forget, those e-mails can be used in the courts if necessary.

I Can Buy Anything I Want on the Web

You can buy many things on the web from virtual shopping malls, but there are two pitfalls: like catalogue shopping, you can't see what you are getting; and some users are still worried about having their credit cards numbers stolen.

CHAPTER 15 ▽ Net myths and reality

Because of this, online shopping has been slow to take off, but there are still hundreds of places to shop, covering everyone from Great Universal to The Body Shop. For the addresses of some online shops, see Chapter 10.

When you send your credit card number over the Internet, it is vulnerable because your message passes through many computers on the way. That's the way the Internet was built. Rather like the phone system, you don't have a direct connection. Instead you connect to the computer equivalent of a telephone exchange, where it would be easy to 'tap' your e-mail.

The answer is to encrypt your details into an unreadable code, which only the computer at the other end can read. This is called a 'secure' connection: when the other computer asks for security, your browser activates that security automatically. Your browser will also warn you when you are entering or leaving a 'secure' part of the Web site. Encoding these details is not foolproof, and the code can be cracked with effort, but for most thieves it isn't worth it. It's easier to steal your credit card slip in a shop and take your card details from that.

Encryption will improve, and there are already banks on the Net. The volume of Net traffic is so huge that your card details are probably safe. Statistically the problem is tiny compared with mobile phone fraud, shoplifting and forgery, but there is still some risk attached.

Will I get Addicted to the Net and Run Up a Huge Phone Bill?

Hopefully not! Time on the Net is cheaper than you think. First, most ISPs offer local call rate connections from anywhere in the UK. This gets cheaper if you enrol with a discount scheme like BT's 'Friends and Family', which offers a further 10 per cent off the cost of calls to five selected numbers. Make one your ISP's access number, and cut the cost of your calls.

Third, try to surf during off-peak times. The Internet is busier in the evening because American users are surfing too. Access will then be slower, but your phone costs are cheaper.

Lastly, you will make a huge saving by browsing Web sites 'off line':

Offline Browsing for Beginners

Imagine you have a pet robot. You tell it to go to your favourite site in the middle of the night, download the pages you want to see, then hang up the phone. When you want to view those pages that Mr Robot has stored on your hard disk, you can read them at your leisure while keeping phone call costs down.

That's the principle of an offline browser. There are several to choose from, but all of them work as an add-on to your current browser – that is, you download the software, and install it to work with your existing browser.

Eventually you will not notice the difference between browsing while connected to your telephone and scrolling through the pages your browser saved for you. There are drawbacks: this requires a lot of hard disk space, because, unlike the Internet, all the files will be stored on your computer. Also, you are not getting up-to-the-minute information. If you collect information from

```
http://www.cnn.com
```

overnight, it will be old news by the time you read it. The beauty of the web is that it is always changing, and an offline reader just gives you a snapshot.

CHAPTER 15 ▽ Net myths and reality

When their phone bill arrives, however, many people find they can live with these drawbacks. To find out more, visit the sites below.

There's a useful site that collects links to all offline readers at http://www.ozemail.com.au/~duckegg/

NearSite
http://www.evolve.co.uk

Browser Buddy
http://www.softbots.com

Secret Agent
http://www.nildram.co.uk

Isn't There Going to be a Special £500 Computer for Net Access?

Perhaps – several companies, notably British company Acorn, want to build one for home users. When it becomes available, it will connect to your television set. Some American companies are already making Internet-aware kitchen units and light switches. If the Internet keeps growing at 10 per cent per month, eventually every appliance will be connected. Our advice is: don't hold your breath.

Glossary

A

Address: Can be either an address of a place on the Internet or the address of a person.

Analogue port: The standard RJ-11 jack that analogue devices such as phones, fax machines, and modems plug into.

AOL (America OnLine): The world's largest conferencing system.

Archie: A way of finding files over the Internet .

ARPA: Advanced Research Projects Agency.

ARPAnet: Advanced Research Projects Agency network- the forerunner of the Internet.

AUP (Acceptable Use Policy): The official policy statement of a network or a service provider that defines which activities may occur on the network. Some AUPs have strict guidelines on which business applications are permitted.

Authoring tool: A piece of software that creates an HTML document for publication on the World Wide Web.

B

Backbone: A high speed data link that connect lots of different networks.

Glossary

BBS (Bulletin Board System): A computer equivalent of a public notice board.

BOND (Bandwidth ON Demand): In ISDN, the ability to aggregate B channels as the data traffic exceeds preset thresholds.

Boolean search: A type of database search that allows the conditions AND, OR and NOT with key words in order to locate specific information.

BRI (Basic Rate Interface): An ISDN service that consists of two 64 kbps Bearer channels (B channels) and one 16 kbps signalling channel (D channel) referred to as 2B+D.

Bridge: A hardware device used for forwarding data between two networks. Unlike a Router, a bridge is not interested in the address on the remote LAN but only in whether or not the packet should be forwarded.

Browser: A software program that provides an interface to the World Wide Web. Netscape Navigator and Microsoft Internet Explorer are the two most popular.

C

CERN: European Particle Physics Laboratory, where a collective of researchers invented the World Wide Web.

CGI (Common Gateway Interface): The mechanism that allows a Web server to run a program or script (such as a Microsoft Visual Basic program) on the local server and send the output to a Web browser.

Chat: An online conversation.

CIS: CompuServe, a US online conferencing system.

CIX (Compulink Information eXchange): UK-only online conferencing system.

Clients: Computers that request and receive information from servers through the network. On the Web, both servers and clients can be Unix, Microsoft Windows or Apple Macintosh computers.

Conference: An area on CIX where people exchange comments on any given subject. Also called a Forum on CIS and Delphi, and a Newsgroup on Usenet.

D

Dial on demand: A dial-up router function that activates a remote link only when data needs to be sent.

Glossary

Dial up: Connecting to another computer via the telephone lines.

DNS (Domain Name System): A method of translating network host names into addresses. On TCP/IP networks, the Domain Name System provides Internet Protocol (IP) address translation for a given computer's domain name. For instance, DNS would associate a computer name such as `fred.smith.co.uk` with the machine's actual numeric IP address, which always takes the format of `xxx.xxx.xxx.xxx`. This allows users to refer to the domain name that is more common and easier to remember when interacting with a remote computer.

Domain: A group of machines on a network that shares something in common, such as the things they do or their location. Top-level domains include `co.uk` for British commercial organizations, `.com` for American commercial organizations and `.edu` for educational institutions.

Download: Transferring a file from another computer to your computer

Dynamic Bandwidth Allocation: A feature that drops one of two B channels being used for a data connection and automatically gives that channel to an incoming voice call or an outgoing call without disrupting the data connection. When the call is completed, the second B channel is then reassigned to the data connection.

E

E-mail (electronic mail): Exchanging messages from computer to computer – not necessarily on the Internet, but generally accepted to be via the Internet.

Emoticon: Term to describe a icon placed in a message that describes an emotion, for example; the smiley :-)

Eudora: A software program that gets your E-mail off the Internet.

F

FAQ: Frequently asked question.

File server: A computer who's data can be accessed by other computers.

Finger: A service that responds to queries and retrieves user information remotely.

Firewall: Software that restricts traffic to a particular area of a network by filtering all communications that pass through a given computer.

Flame: A strong and inflammatory message delivered by e-mail or public posting on an electronic bulletin board. The most enthusiastic flames are typically reserved for businesses that violate AUPs.

Forum: see Conference.

FTP (File Transfer Protocol): The original and most popular way of transferring files from one system to another on a TCP/IP network. Networks that allow 'anonymous FTP' enable anyone to log on to a system and retrieve files, while other FTP systems require that the user enter a password.

G

Gateway: A computer that moves data from one physical network to another.

Gopher: A simple TCP/IP navigation tool for the Internet that allows you to organize and display information within a hierarchical menu system. Developed at the University of Minnesota, it is based on a menu system for easy browsing.

H

Home page: The introductory page or starting page of any World Wide Web site.

Host: Any computer directly connected to the network. A host is not the same as a server.

Host table: A text file used to resolve host names into numeric addresses to identify hosts on a network.

HTML (HyperText Mark-up Language): The Web's text-based coding system, a scripting language that is used to write World Wide Web pages. Hypertext allows a document to be linked to an unlimited number of other documents on the Web. There are currently four levels of HTML compliance.

HTTP (HyperText Transfer Protocol): This is the transport protocol used when transmitting hypertext documents across the Internet.

▽ **Glossary**

HTTP server: A machine that makes a World Wide Web document available to Internet users.

I

ID: Any name used on line – for example, your e-mail address.

Internet server: A computer that offers applications and information to Internet users.

IP (Internet Protocol): The standard protocol that provides for transmitting blocks of data between hosts identified by fixed-length addresses.

IP address (Internet Protocol address): On a TCP/IP network a 32 bit address that uniquely identifies each computer. The network and the computer are both represented in the sequence of numbers. The IP address has a host component and a network component.

IPX (Internet Packet eXchange): The communications protocol for NetWare that routes messages from one node to another.

ISDN (Integrated Services Digital Network): A type of digital communications service that uses two or more 64-kbps B channels to carry data, digitised voice, or video across digital phone lines at high speeds.

ISP (Internet Service Provider): A commercial company that offers individual access to the Internet.

J

Janet (Joint Academic NETwork): Network connecting UK universities and colleges.

L

LAN (Local Area Network): A collection of computers connected together.

Leased line: A telephone line rented for dedicated access to the Internet.

Log in: The process of getting on line, usually with an ID (effectively your online name) and a password (not the same as your ID).

M

Modem (MOdulator/DEModulator): A device that connects the computer to the phone line and allows the computer to transmit and receive data to and from other modems.

Glossary

Mosaic: A freeware World Wide Web browser that uses a graphical user interface to access and view online hypertext documents. Invented at the National Centre for Supercomputing Applications (NCSA) at the University of Illinois.

MUD (Multi-User Domain): An electronic role-playing (gaming) environment.

Multilink PPP (Multilink Point-to-Point Protocol): A multiconnection protocol that lets you bind the two B channels together for a combined throughput of 128 kbps on a single call. Unlike BONDing, Multilink PPP is implemented in software and requires only that your communications software support the protocol.

N

Name server: A computer running DNS that manages Internet domain names and numeric addresses, resolving the names into addresses.

Net: Abbreviation of the Internet.

NetBIOS (Network Basic Input/Output System): A standard PC network interface that allows users to access network devices such as file servers and print servers.

Netiquette: Rules of good behaviour on the Internet.

Network News Transfer Protocol (News, or NNTP): A TCP/IP protocol that defines how newsgroup messages are posted and transported between services.

Newbie: A new person on the Internet.

Newsgroups: Internet discussion groups found on Usenet on the Internet.

NFS (Network File System): A protocol developed by Sun Microsystems, that uses IP to allow a set of computers to access each other's file systems as if they were local.

NIS (Network Information Services): A set of protocols developed by Sun that identifies hosts and addresses across networks.

NT 1 (Network terminator): A connector that attaches a two-wire ISDN line to a four-wire line so that it can be connected to PCs and terminals.

Glossary

O

ODI (Open Data-Link Interface): A Novell specification used for communication with network adapters.

P

Page: A hypermedia document as viewed through a World Wide Web browser.

PAP (Password Authentication Protocol): A type of authentication accomplished by sending user ID/password pairs between two devices.

Password: The 'key' to an online account – known only by the user and the system administrator.

Perl: A scripting language available free in both Microsoft Windows NT and Unix versions.

Ping (Packet INternet Groper): A program that tests whether a particular host is currently on-line and reachable by sending a request and waiting for a reply.

PPP (Point-to-Point Protocol): A protocol similar to SLIP for the transport of TCP/IP packets on serial lines. It governs the way computers connect to networks over a direct link such as a phone line. PPP is the standard for communications with your Internet service provider, as well as for many remote networking clients.

Protocol: An agreed standard way of computers talking to each other; one computer says one thing and expects a specific answer from another.

R

RARP (Reverse Address Resolution Protocol): A protocol used by a diskless machine to find its IP address at start-up.

RIP (Routing Information Protocol): The protocol that routers use to exchange information regarding the location of different routers on an internetwork.

Router: A self-contained unit or computer that makes decisions about which path Internet traffic will take to reach its destination. A router can also filter network packets in order to restrict traffic in or out of its local network.

Glossary

S

Service provider: Organization offering connections to the Internet (*see* ISP).

Server: A host computer that distributes information on the network and stores data on behalf of the clients directly attached to it. It performs such services as resource allocation and sharing, file printing and file downloading.

SGML (Standard Generalized Mark-up Language): A standard for defining and managing the structure of digital documents. SGML separates a document into three components: the header file, which specifies how the document is to be run on a given system; the document type definition (DTD), which describes the layout of the document's components; and the instance, which contains the actual text. HTML is a subset of this standard.

Sig: A users signature put at the end of a message.

SLIP (Serial Line Internet Protocol): A type of Internet connection that allows the dialler to link to the Internet using standard Internet protocols (TCP/IP) on a normal phone line.

SMTP (Simple Mail Transfer Protocol): Used by mail applications to send and receive e-mail.

Snail mail: Post Office mail.

SNMP (Simple Network Management Protocol): A protocol used to monitor devices across the network.

Spam: Sending the same message to lots of places usually specifically to upset people. Seen as a bad breach of etiquette on the Internet; named after the Monty Python sketch where everyone sings 'spam spam spam spam'.

SPID (Service Profile ID): A unique number assigned by the phone company to an ISDN modem. Depending on the type of service and your provider, a separate SPID may also be assigned to each B channel.

Spoofing: The ability of a router to respond locally to certain network requests in order to avoid the need to establish a link connection to a remote site.

Switch: The device used by a ISDN service provider to connect callers to circuits.

Glossary

T

TCP (Transmission Control Protocol): The part of TCP/IP that defines the transport-level protocol. *See* TCP/IP.

TCP/IP (Transmission Control Protocol/Internet Protocol): A collection of communication protocols that allow dissimilar PCs to speak to one another over a network. It is the main building block of the Internet and was originally developed by the US Department of Defense in the 1970s.

Telnet: The Internet protocol whereby users at local PCs can log onto remote systems and use their resources.

TFTP (Trivial File Transfer Protocol): A standard TCP/IP protocol allowing simple file transfer to and from a remote system.

T1 Lines: High-bandwidth (1.544 Mbps) telephone trunk lines. Many regional backbones use T1 lines and some use faster (44.21 Mbps) T3 lines.

U

UNIX: An operating system that was originally developed by AT&T in the late 1960s. There are many versions of UNIX. Much of the Internet was established on UNIX systems, and UNIX is still often used as a base for large-scale Internet access.

Upload: Sending a file to another computer

URL (Uniform Resource Locator): The naming convention computers use to locate pages or documents on the World Wide Web.

Usenet: A network reachable through the Internet that consists of several thousand discussion groups (called newsgroups), ranging from forums for computer programmers to people who can quote *Monty Python* or *Star Trek* verbatim.

V

V.120: A protocol that allows devices that communicate at speeds of less than 64 kbps to adapt their rates to fill an entire 64 kbps B channel. Many PC communications products require support for the V.120 protocol in order to connect.

Glossary

Veronica (Very Easy Rodent Operated Netwide Index to Computerized Archives): A network service on the web that allows users to search for documents.

W

WAIS (Wide Area Information Servers): A service that allows users to search for information on the Internet.

Web browser: Software such as Mosaic, Netscape Navigator or Microsoft Internet Explorer that shows Web pages on a computer (*see* Browser).

Webmaster: The administrator responsible for the management and often design of a World Wide Web site.

Whois: A name lookup service.

Winsock (Windows sockets interface): An industry standard interface that supports portability across network applications.

World Wide Web (WWW or W3): The graphical part of the Internet. It is a computer architecture that was developed at the European Laboratory for Particle Physics in Geneva, Switzerland (CERN) in 1989. A system that allows a user to search for related 'pages' across the Internet. Originally intended to be used in high-energy physics research, the WWW has evolved into a tool for browsing the Internet. Its hypertext links and retrieval capabilities allow users to access referenced information, including text, sound clips, images and video, by pointing and clicking on references in other documents.

X

X.25: A standard protocol defining the interface between data-terminal equipment and packet-switched data networks.

X.500: A standard that defines E-mail directory services, mostly used in Europe.

Index

100 Hot Websites   78

A2Z   75
abbreviations (Net)   150
Adams, Douglas   53
addiction   156
AFP Sports Report   90
Alta Vista   73, 74
Amazing Environmental
    Organization
    Webdirectory   76
America OnLine   15
anonymous FTP   116
AOL *see* America OnLine
Arachnomania   100
Argus/University of Michigan
    Clearinghouse   76
Ashdown, Paddy   53
Ask Mr Angst   96
atheism   109
Atlantic Records   104
audio   41

B (Bearer) channels
    (ISDN)   25
BABT (British Approvals Board
    for Telecommunications)
    25
BBS *see* bulletin boards
Beatles, The   105
Beavis and Butthead   53
Bible Gateway   90
Bigfoot   51
books   91
Books On-Line   91
broadcasting   119
browser, anatomy   43
Browser Buddy   162
browsing   68
bulletin boards (BBS)   13
business   93
business Newsgroups   63
buying on the Web   159

café.internet   23

Index

CareerNet UK 101
CareerWeb 101
CCTA Government
   Information 103
CD World 105
Channel 4 109
Christian Introduction to the
   Web 109
Cinemania OnLine 109
CIS *see* Compuserve
CIX *see* Compulink
   Information Exchange
Clancy, Tom 53
Classic CD 104
Clinton, Bill 53
clock speed 33
CNN Interactive 106
comedy 95
ComedyWeb 95
Comparative Religion 109
compression (modem) 24
Compulink Information
   Exchange 16
Compuseve 15
computing 97
computing Newsgroups 61
Conservative Party, The 103
Content Filters 155
copyright 145, 154
culture 98
Cupid's Network 107
CU-SeeMe 118
CV writing *see* résumé
   writing
CyberPatrol 156
CyberSitter 156

D (Delta) channels (ISDN) 25
Dateline UK 89, 107
Dear Xavier Landers 96
Dejanews 52, 76
Digital Signal Processors 42
Discovery Channel
   Online 100
dot pitch 41
downloading software 112
Dr Solomon's 117
DSP *see* Digital Signal

Processors

Educate Online 100
education 99
Electric Library 74
Electronic Newsstand 106
Electronic Telegraph 89, 106
e-mail 13, 48, 120
   addresses 50, 53
   Netiquette 146
   responding to messages 58
   sending 49
e-mail reader, anatomy 46
Emoticons 150
employment 101
encryption 160
Entertainment Online 102
ESPN SportZone 110
Excite 77
Explorer (Microsoft) 30

fallback speed (modem) 24
FAQ (frequently asked
   questions) 147
FIFA Online 110
File Transfer Protocol
   (FTP) 115
film 107
Financial Times 81 *see also*
   ft.com
'flaming' 146
F-Prot 118
ft.com 70, 94
FTP *see* File Transfer Protocol
FTP sites 118

Gamelan 77
games 102
Games Domain, The 86, 102
Gamespot 102
gaming 17
Gates, Bill 48, 53
Gere, Richard 11
GM (General MIDI)
   standard 42
GNN Select 77
G.O.D. (Global Online
   Directory) 77

Index

government 103
Gradunet 84, 101
Grisham, John 53
Grodin, Charles 53
Guardian OnLine 106

hackers 158
hard disk 36
hardware
  essentials 31
  supplier installation 42
HarperCollins Interactive 92
Hayes command set 25
hobbies Newsgroups 61
home page 66
Hoskins, Bob 53
hotlinks 10
Hotbot 78
HotDog 119
HTML 133
  introduction 133

IBM Infomarket 78
Id Software 102
Idol, Billy 53
images Newsgroups 64
Infoseek Guide 78
Intel 34
Interactive Frog
  Dissection 100
Interactive TV Guide 107
Internet
  component parts 8
  definitions 1, 8
  is it for you? 1
  multimedia
requirements 32
Internet Beatles album and
  Beatles info 105
Internet Bookshop 81, 91
Internet Browsrs 28
Internet Cafés 22
Internet for Learning 100
Internet Movie database 108
Internet News 12, 45, 55, 57,
  59, 62, 148
Internet Public Library 91
Internet Talking Bookshop 92

Internet Telephony 128
Investor's Edge 93
IRC 17, 125
ISDN (Integrated Sevices
  Digital Network) 21,
  25

Java 77
Jobs in the UK 101
Joke of the Day 95
jokes Newgroups 63
Judo Resources 69

Keillor, Garrison 53

Labour Party, The 103
Landers, Xavier see Dear
  Xavier Landers
laws on the Internet 153
leased lines 22, 25
Led Zeppelin 13
Liberal Democratic Party,
  The 103
Light Bulb Jokes 96
Literary Calendar 99
LookUp 52
Loot 82, 93
Louvre, The 99
Lycos 75

Magellan 75
mailing lists 122
  joining 123
Man is Man Made 109
Match.com 107
McAfee 118
memory 36
Microsoft 98
Microsoft Network 15
Microsoft web site 30, 67
MIDI (Musical Instrument Data
  Interface) 42
Migraine Boy 96
modems 20, 23
  connection to your PC 26
money 93
MoneyWorld UK 95

Index

monitor 40
Mosaic (Spry) 29
Movie Database 85
MPEG video 40
Mr Angst *see* Ask Mr Angst
Mr Showbiz 109
MSN *see* Microsoft Network
MSNBC 105
MTV Online 88, 104
MUD *see* Multi-User Dungeon
Multi-User Dungeon 18
Murray Walker Quotes 10
music 104

National Museum of Film, Photography and Television 98
Navigator (Netscape) 30
NearSite 162
Nerdworld Media Internet Subject Index 78
Net
 basics 19
 history 6
 uses 4
Net access, cheap 160
Net addiction 160
Net myths and reality 153
Netiquette 146–152
 abbreviations 150
 basics 147
 e-mail 149
 Emoticons 150
Newsgroups 147
 Smileys 150–152
 spam 149
NetNanny 156
New Scientist (Planet Science) 84, 99
news reader, anatomy 45
news servers 56, 57
Newsgroups 11, 54, 124, 147
 business 63
 computing 61
 hobbies 61
 images 64
 jokes 63
 sport 62

starters 61
threads 55
trivia 62
UK-specific 62
newspapers 105
NME (NME.com) 87, 104
Norton AntiVirus 118
Numbering Rule 33, 34
NUS Online 100

offline browsing
 beginners 161
Online Career Centre 101
online services 15
Open Text Index 79
Overdrive (Intel) 35

PA News 106
Paramount Pictures 85, 108
Pastel Blue 105
Pathfinder 104
Pentium (Intel) 34
Pentium Pro (Intel) 34
People Bank 94
peptide newsgroup 13
Perot, Ross 53
personals 107
Philip K.Dick 93
Planet Science *see* New Scientist
Point 79
pornography 154
Pratchett, Terry 53
Prentice Hall 92
processor 33
processor upgrade 35
Pulp Faction 93
Pytholine 95

radio 107
Random Access Memory (RAM) *see* memory
Real Time 17
Recreational Software Advisory Council (RSAC) 156, 157
religion 109
résumé (CV) writing 95

Index

Reuter's Business
   Headlines 94
Riddler (riddler.com) 86, 102
RSAC *see* Recreational
   Software Advisory
   Council

Santa Claus 53
screenplay writing
   Newsgroup 13
Search Engines 71
Secret Agent 162
Shakespeare 99
Shareware (shareware.com)
   76, 97, 114
Shoppers Universe 93
shopping 155
Short Cuts 144
sig 148
Smileys 150–152
Smithsonian Institution 83, 98
Soccernet 91, 111
software
   anatomy 43
   downloading 112
   locating 114
   virus detection 117, 118
software (free) 113
   anonymous FTP 115
   disadvantages 116
   searching 114
Spam Club 82
spam, spamming 149
Spawn 92
Spin Magazine 105
Spirit-WWW 110
sport 110
sport Newsgroups 62
Sports Chat! 111
Star Trek 108
Starsky and Hutch 9
Starting Point 79
SurfWatch 156
Sydney 2000 111

T1 (leased) line 26
T3 (leased) line 26

tags (HTML) 134
Telegraph, The *see* Electronic
   Telegraph
threads *see* Newsgroups
Times, The 106
Travel Books 93
trivia Newsgroups 62
TV 107

UART (Universal
   Asynchronous Receiver
   Transmitter) Chip 28
   older PCs 27
UK Business Index 94
UK Club Map 99
UK Internet Directory 97
UK-specific Newsgroups 62
Universal Asynchronous
   Receiver Transmitter *see*
   UART Chip
University of Michigan
   Clearinghouse *see* Argus
URL (Universal Resource
   Location) 10
Usenet 11, 54
   discussion 55
   exploring 59
   free speech 60
   posting a message 56
   workings 56

Vatican Radio 110
Versions 97
video 37
Videoconferencing 128
Virgin Radio 105
viruses 117, 159
VMPeg 118
VRAM (Video Random Access
   Memory) 38

W3 Servers 79
Walker, Murray *see* Murray
   Walker Quotes
Wall Street Journal 94
Wall-o-shame 96
Web beginning 65, 66

Index

Web Pages
  content 131, 145
  how they work 132
  making your own 131
Web Sites 80–111
Webcrawler 79
What's New 79
White House, The 87, 103
Whowhere? 79
World Sports Report 110
World Wide Web 9

WWW Bible Gateway 109

Xavier Landers *see* Dear Xavier Landers

Yahoo! UK and Ireland 72, 74

ZDNet 97
Ziff Davis *see* ZDNet

Licensing Agreement

This book comes with a CD software package. By opening this package, you are agreed to be bound by the following:

The software contained on this CD is, in many cases, copyrighted, and all rights are reserved by the individual licensing agreements associated with each piece of software contained on the CD. THIS SOFTWARE IS PROVIDED FREE OF CHARGE, AS IS, AND WITHOUT WARRANTY OF ANY KIND, EITHER EXPRESSED OR IMPLIED, INCLUDING, BUT NOT LIMITED TO THE IMPLIED WARRANTIES OF MERCHANTABILITY AND FITNESS FOR A PARTICULAR PURPOSE. Neither the book publisher nor it's dealers and distributors assumes any liability for any alleged or actual damages arising from the use of this software.